Great Jewish
Debates and Dilemmas

Great Jewish Debates and Dilemmas

JEWISH PERSPECTIVES IN CONFLICT IN THE EIGHTIES

Albert Vorspan

UNION OF AMERICAN HEBREW
CONGREGATIONS · NEW YORK, N.Y.

LIBRARY OF CONGRESS CATA-
LOGING IN PUBLICATION DATA

Vorspan, Albert.
Great Jewish debates and
    dilemmas.

1. Judaism and social problems
—Addresses, essays, lectures.
2. Jews—Politics and government—1948–   —Addresses,
essays, lectures. I. Title.
HN40.J5V58 296.3'87 80–21057
ISBN 0–8074–0049–1

MANUFACTURED IN THE U.S. OF AMERICA
1 2 3 4 5 6 7 8 9 0

This book is dedicated to the memory of I. CYRUS GORDON who served for many years as chairman of the Commission on Social Action of Reform Judaism.

I have never known a man who was so gentle and warm-hearted but—at the same time—so filled with indignation and disquiet in the face of injustice. He was a beloved friend and co-worker, an exceptional mentsch, and a living testimony to the power of the engaged Jewish conscience.

Contents

Rabbis Must Define Their Obligations
No Separate Congregations

Foreword

I want to express my appreciation to Rabbi Daniel B. Syme, director of education, for playing the Jewish mother in nudging me to write this book in the first place and for his skilled criticism and valued suggestions; to Rabbi Doug Kahn, then a rabbinical student; to Rabbi Daniel Polish of the Synagogue Council of America; Rabbi David Saperstein, of the Religious Action Center; and Rabbi Balfour Brickner, director of Interreligious Activities of the UAHC, for their helpful and knowledgeable comments; to Ruth Harrison, for miraculously deciphering my hieroglyphics and chicken scratches and for typing the drafts in her uniquely efficient and complaining manner; to Ralph Davis, UAHC's long-time resident genius production manager, for fashioning a handsome book out of my manuscript; to Eric Feldheim, who did the final editing so capably; to Francine Charley, secretary at Temple Beth-El of Great Neck, for giving freely her time for the final typing; and to my wife and four children who didn't have a blessed thing to do with this book, but who think it is splendid.

Preface

Once—a mere decade or two ago—it seemed so easy to make a clear moral judgment on the big issues in American society. It seemed so easy to tell the good guys from the bad, to stand up and be counted. It did not require great sophistication to distinguish between helpless Black children in Birmingham being assaulted by police dogs, fire hoses, and electric cattle prods and the goons who attacked them. It was not hard to see the virtue in those who sought to achieve the elementary right to vote—and to condemn those who sought to frustrate that right. It was easy to criticize those who invoked censorship against free speech or free assembly. It was harder to make a judgment on our Vietnam War, but most Americans finally saw it as a morally disastrous enterprise.

But the hard, clear-cut issues of yesteryear have, somehow, faded into the complex and shadowy dilemmas of today. Racial justice is still a high moral goal, but which methods—affirmative action, busing, quotas—are right and which are wrong? And who says so, by what authority, and under what circumstances? Censorship is bad, yes, but do American Nazis have a right to march in uniforms in a community made up largely of Holocaust survivors? The certainties of yesterday too often become the uncertainties and conflicts of today, including those in which one right collides with another right to bedevil our contemporary society.

This is true for all Americans; for Jews only more so. Why? When the Shah was toppled in Iran, it became a problem for every American, for the Shah had been created in our image and had become central to our foreign policy. But for Jews there was a special dilemma! The Shah had been a despot, but he had also protected the 70,000 Iranian Jews and was a strong oil and trade partner with Israel. Our Jewish dilemma, as usual, had a particular bite, as it does also in Skokie and in such issues as abortion, the rights of women and homosexuals, energy and ecology, the SALT treaty, relations with the Soviet Union, and South Africa. Add the questions raised by affirmative action, the rights of Palestinians, and the size of the defense budget, and you may well ask: How do we balance the often conflicting claims of Jewish ethics and Jewish interests confronting our Jewish conscience? That is the subject of this book.

What is the *Jewish* dimension in these issues? What is the Jewish stake? If Jewish tradition speaks to these conflicts, it does not always do so clearly and directly. There is no "Thou shalt" and "Thou shalt not" of ancient Sinai. There are no easy answers to such many-sided complexities, not anymore, not in the America of the eighties.

But the open-ended and muddled nature of these issues does not exempt us Jews from facing their moral challenges. We may have to balance gingerly on moral tightropes, but we cannot escape our Jewish mission. With greater modesty and less certainty than in the past, with more tentativeness and greater tolerance for dissenting views, we still carry the Jewish burden we have carried through the corridors of an anguished history: to face this world and its pain head on; to engage in endless study and moral debate; to cherish human life and to pursue justice; to enhance the life of the mind and to struggle, despite all complexity and despair, to be God's co-partners in repairing His broken and incomplete world. It was never easy, even in the old days; it is more difficult today and will be even harder tomorrow. But, if the agenda is more complex today, our duty to do the right thing on this earth is as compelling as ever.

Editor's Introduction

Every era reflects its own unique set of challenges to the nobility of the human spirit. Profound issues confront us with difficult and painful choices, and we, as individuals and as a community, ultimately are known by the choices we make.

As we enter the 1980s, it is apparent that the Jewish community faces a world in which the historical tension between universalism and particularism will be sharper, and perhaps more wrenching, than ever before in recent history.

In *Great Jewish Debates and Dilemmas: Jewish Perspectives in Conflict in the Eighties,* Albert Vorspan tackles the tough issues, the issues that have the potential to either divide our society or unite us in common purpose. Presenting both sides of every dilemma, and setting each one in a Jewish context, Vorspan puts before us such questions as race relations, civil liberties, energy, religious freedom, Israel, and crime and punishment. Where do we stand? What are we prepared to do?

Jewish Debates and Dilemmas represents yet another major contribution by Albert Vorspan to the literature of Jewish social action. A champion of justice and human dignity, his writings have touched the hearts and minds of tens of thousands of Jews of all ages. This latest volume, in the tradition of *Jewish Values and Social Crisis,* brings his hard-hitting analysis and special sensitivity to a whole new generation of high school and adult students. We hope that you will find this volume meaningful and helpful in your personal search for Jewish responses to pressing social concerns.

Rabbi Daniel B. Syme

Introduction

This book succeeds my long-standing *Jewish Values and Social Crisis*. The main difference between that earlier volume and this one is the sharply contrasting spirit of the sixties versus the eighties. The moral issues that seemed so clear-cut in the 1960s—race, war and peace, affirmative action, civil liberties, church-state separation, social welfare—have now blurred into the complex dilemmas of the 1980s. It would be presumptuous to suggest that Judaism points clear answers to the great debates of our time; it doesn't. Good and sensitive Jews—and others—are on both sides of many of these honest controversies. Nonetheless, the historic ethical traditions of Judaism do offer sharp insights and wise perspectives in helping us to evaluate the issues which challenge our era.

But Judaism does not permit us to cop out in despair, fatigue, or because of the complexity of the issues. It commands us to take this battered world in our hands and to put it on the anvil of life—and beat it into human shape. Rabbi Tarphon, the ancient sage, said: "The hour is late. The Master is urgent. It is not incumbent upon us to complete the task, but neither are we free to desist from it." If this book stirs some of us to confront our dilemmas and to strive for a better world, dayenu . . . that would be sufficient gratification for the author.

1

RACE RELATIONS

In the summer of 1979, Black-Jewish relations in the United States, already strained, came close to a breaking point. What brought the pot to a boil was the Andrew Young affair. Andrew Young, vigorous United States ambassador to the United Nations, was the highest ranking Black in the Carter Administration; no Black person ever had the ear of a president as did Andrew Young.

In July of 1979, Ambassador Young attended a meeting at the New York home of the Kuwaiti ambassador. There he met with an official PLO representative with whom he discussed a pending United Nations resolution. By so doing, Ambassador Young had clearly violated an explicit commitment by the United States not to enter into contact with the PLO unless and until that terrorist organization had accepted UN Resolutions 242 and 238; these two resolutions deal, among other matters, with Israeli troop withdrawal from Arab territories and the right to peaceful existence of *all* states in the area including, of course, the State of Israel.

That pledge had been written into the Sinai disengagement treaty between Israel, Egypt, and the United States. A news magazine got wind of the Young visit and asked if it had really happened. Ambassador Young issued a "cover" story, stating that it had been an accidental social visit only. Thereafter, Young went to the Israeli ambassador, told him the true story, and urged Israel not to make a public protest of this matter lest it inflame the American Black community and generate support for the PLO in the United States. The Israelis, however, felt compelled to protest, making the issue public. Jewish leaders responded with fury to the revelation that the US had violated its clear pledge to Israel not to meet with the PLO. One Jewish leader demanded that Young be fired; all others saw the Young meeting as part of an Administration shift towards recognition of the PLO—a policy which they felt Ambassador Young was merely implementing when he was caught.

In the storm of controversy, Ambassador Young resigned. Immediately, rage and bitterness exploded among Black leaders. Many blamed the Israelis and American Jews for bringing down Andrew Young. One Black accused the Israelis of deliberately setting out to humiliate America's leading Black, another accused Jews of disloyalty to America. Jews responded that it was not a matter of color, but one of policy; that Ambassador Young had been fired because he had violated US policy and had lied to his superiors in the State Department; and that Blacks in their anger were now using Jews as scapegoats.

Thereafter, several leaders of the Southern Christian Leadership Conference held a meeting with PLO representatives and announced that they would support "Palestinian rights" to a "Homeland" of their own. Jews, in turn, reacting angrily, denounced efforts to put a mantle of respectability on Arab terrorists. They warned that Blacks were being diverted from their own vital domestic concerns of jobs, housing, welfare reform, and inflation—concerns which Jews, more than any others, share. The wounding confrontation confirmed the worst instincts of people in both groups. Many Jews took the affair as evidence that Blacks are anti-Jewish; many Blacks took the affair to mean that Jews control America. It was a tragedy of major proportions.

HUMAN RIGHTS AND JEWISH TRADITION

Of all the great issues of our times, perhaps none evokes a stronger resonance from Jewish teaching than the search for human rights. Contrary to the vicious lie of a 1975 UN resolution, declaring Zionism to be a form of racism and racial discrimination, Jewish tradition emphatically rejects all notions of racial superiority.

Judaism gave to the world the concept of the sanctity and dignity of the individual. All people are equal because they are created in the image of God. Respect for the civil rights of others is each person's duty to God. "What is hateful to you, do not do to your neighbor." (Babylonian Talmud, Shabbat 8)

In the Midrash (Bereshit Rabbah) it is asked: Why did God create one man, Adam? The answer is illuminating. "Man was created one so that no one can say, 'My father was greater than your father'." The major aim of synagogue social action and of Jewish community relations is the protection and enhancement of equal rights and equal opportunities for all persons and the creation of conditions that contribute toward vital Jewish living. The security of the Jewish group, as of all groups, rests on the foundation of democratic freedoms of full equality, of individual rights, and of personal liberties for all, without regard to race or religion.

Jews have been in the forefront of the struggle to achieve equality of opportunity for the Black, the Hispanic, the Oriental, and members of all groups suffering from discrimination. There is a growing recognition that, not only anti-Semitism, but discrimination against any racial or religious group in American life threatens the ultimate security of the Jew. More important for our purposes is the view that Judaism, to fulfill itself, must exert the full weight of its moral prestige towards the achievement of equality by all persons, regardless of race or national origin. For this principle is the essence of our religious faith as it is the essence of democracy itself.

The term "civil rights," as used in this book, refers to the inherent right of *every* citizen to equality of opportunity. The area of "civil liberties," designated freedoms of speech, assembly, press, and others, will be taken up in a later chapter. While these two areas are related, each has had in recent years a markedly different development.

Thus, it is not surprising that American Jews responded powerfully to the fight against racial segregation in America. After all, no other group has been so frequently the victim of racial hatred, as the Jewish people itself. Jews, more than any other segment of the white population, played an active role in the dramatic civil rights struggles of the fifties and sixties, when the Black-Jewish alliance was at the heart of the civil rights movement.

When the Mississippi Summer of 1964 was organized to break the back of legal segregation in the then most stubbornly resistant state of the Union, more than half of the young people who volunteered from all parts of the US were Jewish youngsters. Two of the three martyrs of that struggle, killed by mobs in Philadelphia, Mississippi, were Jewish; the third was Black. Most of the funds raised by such organizations as the National Association for the Advancement of Colored People, the Southern Christian Leadership Conference and the Student Non-Violent Coordinating Committee came from Jews. Rabbis marched with Martin Luther King throughout the south; many were jailed; some were beaten. Jewish political leverage contributed to passage of landmark civil rights laws, nationally and locally.

True, the moral issues were obvious. Could Judaism fail to distinguish between non-violent Blacks seeking the elementary right to vote, or to be treated without discrimination in a hotel, a store or a restaurant, and the mobs which attacked them with police dogs, cattle prods, high-pressure hoses, and even rifles? Was it difficult to choose Martin Luther King over Bull Connor, segregationist police chief of Birmingham? Not all Jews were willing to stand up and be counted, but there was no question where Judaism—and most Jews—had to stand. Compared to today, the line between right and wrong was then simple to draw.

Today the issues of right and wrong in the continuing quest for racial decency are often confused, ambiguous, and controversial. Good men and women are on both sides of such thorny issues as affirmative action and the wisdom of long-distance busing to achieve racial integration. For, it is now clear, desegregating a small southern town in the sixties was easy compared to the mammoth effort required to desegregate a vast northern city—like New York or Philadelphia—with all the attendant problems of white flights to the suburbs, decaying schools, declining tax revenues, crime and violence, and the shrinking quality of public education.

AFFIRMATIVE ACTION

One issue in the realm of race relations has risen to the level of great debate: affirmative action. As civil rights laws of major dimensions were passed in the sixties, it became clear that it was not enough merely to pass laws prohibiting discrimination against Blacks. Society had to do something positive to make amends for centuries of past injury to racial minorities. Congress mandated "affirmative action," requiring colleges, employers, and government agencies to reach out in positive steps to bring long-deprived members of minority groups into the mainstream of American life. Implicit in this effort is the idea that it is not enough for a professional school, for example, to say from now on we will accept anybody without discrimination; millions of Americans are handicapped by generations of poor schooling, unfair treatment, and blatant inequality. Action is required to redress the balance.

Thus, affirmative action programs mushroomed in all phases of life. And, inevitably, conflicts about its implications simmered and exploded.

Many white Americans felt that special treatment for minorities meant reverse discrimination against themselves and their children. Protest and anger swelled into legal challenges and public opinion tilted against racial preferences in affirmative action. Blacks felt betrayed and cheated of the opportunity to make something of themselves in an America which seemed to be turning its back on the goal of full equality. When unemployment reached Depression levels within the Black community, particularly among young Blacks, 40 percent of whom were jobless in some cities, fuel was added to the gathering fire of anger and resentment.

The lightning rod and the symbol of the mounting controversy about affirmative action was the landmark legal case of Alan Bakke. Bakke, a white Protestant male had applied for admission to the medical school of the University of California at Davis. He was already 34 years of age, a factor which may have contributed to his rejection by twelve other medical schools, despite his good grades and strong motivation to be a doctor. At Davis he was also rejected. He blamed the affirmative action program of the school. In order to enroll more Blacks, Asians, women, and American Indians, Davis had developed a two-track admission system. In one track, 16 places were reserved for qualified members of minority groups. While qualified to be medical students, these applicants had grade averages considerably lower than those admitted into the general admissions program. Mr. Bakke, who was rejected, had higher grades than most of those accepted in the special track.

Bakke went to court, charging "reverse discrimination." He contended that he had been excluded from the Davis Medical School because he was white and that this was a violation of his constitutional rights. The university argued that it had the legal right to develop the dual admission system to overcome historic inequalities and to bring persons of deprived background into the student body.

The Bakke case snaked its way to the Supreme Court and it became a major cause for the breakup of the old civil rights coalition. It sharply divided the Jewish community and Black civil rights organization. Major Jewish groups, including the American Jewish Congress, the American Jewish Committee, and the Anti-Defamation League, submitted arguments to the

US Supreme Court in behalf of Bakke. Their briefs argued that what the Davis Medical School had created was nothing less than a quota system—a rigid, inflexible, numerical system which preferred one group to another. They pointed out that, historically, Jews had had much bitter experience with quota systems in czarist Russia, in early periods of American life, and elsewhere in their long history. Quotas, they argued, were unfair and unconstitutional. They treated persons solely as representatives of *groups* (Blacks, women, Asians, etc.) rather than as individuals entitled to individual rights. The Constitution does not protect *group* rights, only *individual* rights. Indeed, if people are judged only as groups, it might follow that Jews could be accused of being overrepresented in colleges and professional schools.

Moreover, they contended, who is to say what groups are entitled to special privilege? Why not Jews, Poles, Italians, or Hispanics? And, where is it written that a person is automatically deprived merely because he or she is Black? The child of a prosperous Black lawyer, is no more deprived than is the white next-door neighbor. A Jew, an Italian, or a Greek may have grown up in a slum or in a broken home or have come from persecution in Europe. Therefore, let affirmative action be exerted for individuals—regardless of color, religion, or ancestry—who have suffered actual deprivation and who are, therefore, entitled to a special hand. But, let the state and the school and the employer be colorblind; otherwise, the old racial injustice will be replaced by a new form of reverse discrimination.

Civil rights activists went to court in support of the university; they rejected the arguments made in behalf of Bakke. They pointed out that, prior to the creation of a special program by Davis, the medical school was virtually all white and all male. Without a special effort to reach out and provide remedial help, there would never be diversity in the student body. They pointed out that America's Black inner cities and rural ghettoes needed Black doctors if decent medical services were ever to be delivered to the Black poor. They argued that affirmative action on the college and professional school level was succeeding, as shown by the growing number of minority doctors, lawyers, and engineers. They emphasized that it is not equality to bring everyone to the starting gate to compete in a race in which minority youngsters are crippled by a history of inferior schooling, bad housing, and demoralizing treatment. Nor, they claim, is it a matter of individual rights. Blacks as a race were enslaved, mistreated, and cheated by society. Blacks as a group suffered deprivation, and the total society must redress these past grievances by genuine affirmative action. It is in the strongest public interest to overcome the ugly heritage of the past and to bring the disadvantaged into the mainstream of American life.

The Supreme Court eventually ruled in favor of Bakke, ordering the university to admit him, on the ground that his constitutional rights had been violated. It held the university's two-track system illegal because the minority students only had to compete against each other and were not made to compete against all other applicants in the pool. They characterized the system of reserving places as a "quota" which was not permissible under law.

In a closely divided vote (5 to 4), the Justices also affirmed the validity of affirmative action programs which avoided the flaws of Cal/Davis. They stated that race could properly be taken into consideration as one factor along with a host of other reasons such as geography, grades, personality, motivation, and economic background. The Supreme Court reached a compromise in its decision seeking to strike down the excesses without weakening the heart of affirmative action.

In a later case, Weber vs. Kaiser, a white worker went to court to fight an affirmative action program developed voluntarily by a labor union and the Kaiser Company to qualify workers for skilled trades. Black groups defended the program. The Anti-Defamation League took Weber's side; other Jewish groups stayed out. The Supreme Court upheld the voluntary plan as constitutional. When the Andrew Young controversy developed, some Black leaders accused Jews of being among the most determined opponents of affirmative action, thus becoming "defenders of the racial status quo."

Discussion about affirmative action should not blind us to the real condition of American Blacks. Among Black adults the rate of unemployment is double of what it is among white workers; for Black teenagers the rate is three times that of white young men and women. A Black male with a college degree earns an annual income of just about $110 more than a white male high school graduate. Blacks are approximately 11.5 percent of our total population, but they comprise only 1.2 percent of lawyers and judges, 2 percent of physicians, 2.3 percent of dentists, 1.1 percent of engineers, and 2.6 percent of college and university professors. As Justice Marshall said in his angry dissent in the Bakke case, "At every point from birth to death, the impact of the past is reflected in the still disfavored position of the Negro." In a shrinking job market, the chances of a Black person working his or her way out of poverty and despair are very bleak, indeed.

Even the most far-reaching affirmative action programs would barely scratch the surface of our most serious racial problems. Gunnar Myrdal, in his book, *An American Dilemma,* put the challenge squarely: "You are cutting off an underclass which is not needed, not employable. . . . You must create out of this underclass, or their children at least, human beings who fit into modern America, who are needed, who are productive, who have a value. This is what the question is all about."

Even now, America has failed to reclaim that lost generation. Many Black youngsters of 13 and 14 have little or no future in America. An entire generation of minority youth finds itself in decaying slums and failing schools, in hopeless unemployment, and dependent on an inhumane welfare system. Many of these young people feel that they do not count and there is no place for them in America. Many inevitably end up hustling on the street, the training ground for serious crime.

They fight for survival in a society in which half of all Black children are born out of wedlock, and many live in poor and fatherless homes, forced to subsist on welfare. A study of

Watts, the Black ghetto of Los Angeles, concludes that crime is often the major single source of income for ghetto youth. This waste of a generation is not only a human disaster, but it creates a society where no one is safe. History shows that Jews have most to fear from an angry and convulsed society. Recent events, such as the Andrew Young affair, prove again that, in an atmosphere of tension, Blacks, or any others, tend to blame the Jews for their misfortune.

INTEGRATION AND QUALITY EDUCATION

In the 1950s and 1960s, racial integration was not only a national goal, it was also clearly seen as a moral imperative. Thus, members of the three major faiths, Protestants, Catholics, and Jews, played prominent roles in the massive effort to end segregated schooling in America, recognizing the truth of the Supreme Court's verdict that "separate but equal is inherently unequal."

Now, after two decades of experience, the question seems no longer is it right or is it wrong, but rather how to best achieve the stated goal. Chief among the questions are: Do minority students learn better in desegregated schools? Does desegregation accelerate white flight? Is the extent of white flight related to the sweep of the integration plan? Does integration make for better feelings among groups or does it cause increased conflict? Does desegregation of schools lead to closer personal relations across racial lines? Can integration be achieved wihout uniting city and suburb?

The answers are shrouded in ambiguity. If it was possible in the early civil rights days to separate the "good guys" from the "bad guys" by where they stood on racial integration, today men and women of good will are often divided on these troublesome questions and scholars are equally uncertain.

The effects of desegregation on scholastic achievement are also in doubt. Some experts who first held that academic improvement for minority students required desegregation have also produced studies indicating that racial desegregation has had only a minor effect on the test scores of minority students. Other scholars disagree. Most experts, however, agree that the gap between Black and white students can best be overcome when desegregated schooling begins at an early age, preferably by second grade. When students are moved after junior high school, their scores may actually decline.

Research on the atmosphere in desegregated schools is equally disturbing; race frequently is the dominant factor how students cluster in the cafeteria, the classroom, and on the playing field. Merely putting youngsters in the same school does not ensure genuine integration.

The question of "white flight" is central to a discussion of race relations. A study by Dr. James S. Coleman in 1975 reported that white flight was so massive in some cases that desegregation could be obliterated within a few years. Dr. Christine H. Rossell had concluded: "The greater the school desegregation, the greater the white loss." She also found that widespread busing into formerly all-Black schools resulted in a doubled rate of white flight. On the other hand, where Blacks are bused into formerly all-white areas, little white loss results.

The many questions which arise from the desegregation process require constant study and continued work. But all this should not obscure the fundamental truth that America is the only nation which, despite a history of racial arrogance and slavery, has risen to break the back of legal segregation, to pave the way for a truly open, free, and multi-racial society. We have heavy lifting to do to achieve this goal, but we have already come a long distance. And, no current travail can diminish the moral grandeur of this victory.

JEWS AND BLACKS

Jewish behavior on race is full of dilemmas and ambivalences. Judaism, as a religious tradition, rejects racism; but Jews as individuals are as prone to racial bigotry as other people. Many

Jews are sensitive to the impact of discrimination through their own history, but some Jews are also slum landlords and merchants who exploit poor people. Jews rarely resort to violence or overt meanness when Blacks or Hispanics move into the neighborhood; but Jews and other Americans have left the cities in a massive post-World War II exodus, moving to suburbs which are usually all-white, turning many parts of our cities into Black ghettoes.

Did we run away from the Blacks? Most would deny it, citing instead the deteriorating public schools in the city and the green grass and fresh air in the suburbs. But, our behavior demonstrates that we believe in integration in the abstract but prefer a style of living which is "separate but better."

Jewish attitudes toward public education often reflect the same dilemmas. Jews have had a honeymoon with American public education; that system afforded the push which lifted a poor immigrant community into one of the most upwardly mobile and successful minority groups in the history of America. But, today that honeymoon has turned sour. Increasingly, Jews who remain in the city feel compelled to put their children into private schools. Indeed, the rising Jewish interest in Jewish day schools stems, in part, from a desire to escape the impact of busing and integration on the quality and safety of public schools.

Are Jews abandoning public education? The overwhelming majority of Jewish youngsters still attend public schools. Where public schools have declined in quality and are marred by violence or tension, Jewish parents cannot be expected to sacrifice their child's education on the altar of high principle. But, what is good for Jewish parents is obviously good for non-Jewish parents, too, provided they can afford the exorbitant cost of private schools. Where does all that leave the future of public education? Perhaps as a dumping ground for poor non-whites—a school for children left behind in the mass flight to suburbia or to the sanctuaries of private schools. In the long run, is such a prospect good for America? Is it good for Jews? Is it good for anybody?

The mass middle-class withdrawal from our cities has also distorted Black-Jewish relations in America. But, there are many other factors as well. In the 1950s and 1960s, civil rights were an appealing moral cause for many white liberals, including Jews, because it had to do with obvious injustices in faraway communities. The right of Blacks to vote in Mississippi was sincerely supported by all fair-minded people. Many Jews actively led that effort to rectify blatant discrimination. In those years, anti-discrimination laws were also seen as breaking down remaining discrimination against Jews and others in housing, employment, and other aspects of American life.

But when integration came to one's own town in the North—and into one's own schools—Jews behaved as emotionally as anyone else. When Los Angeles, California, was ordered by the courts to institute long-distance busing to correct a pattern of racial segregation in the schools, Jews were vocal and visible in the leadership of the outraged opposition. One local rabbi was severely castigated by his congregants when he compared this opposition to the racism which had once been so notorious in the South. Is it racism to oppose busing for integration? Is it racism to believe that racial integration has failed to improve public education? One Black leader has said that the tumult about busing is not really about transportation. "It ain't the bus," he said, "it's us." Ironically, some Los Angeles parents, after condemning busing as evil, often put their children into day schools, to which they were, of course, then taken on long-distance buses.

Thus, racial justice for many Jews is no longer a moral obligation or a cause to help some Blacks somewhere else. To many, it is now seen as a direct threat to good education, to safety, to property values, to the quality of life. Jews once derived great self-esteem from the sense of benevolence extended to Black people. Now, many Jews see Blacks as competitors for scarce jobs as teachers or social workers and the limited places in graduate schools. It is probably correct to say that Black-Jewish relations were never as good, even in the old days, as we retrospectively romanticize them to have been. They inherently were unequal, not peer to peer. We Jews provided much of the expertise, the legal resources, and the leadership. This subordinate role is now rejected by a Black community, weary of being patronized and determined to take control of its own destiny. That displaced many Jews, some of whom felt betrayed. It was a healthy and overdue revolt against condescension, but it also led too often to excesses of Black separatism, further estranging Blacks and Jews.

As Jews abandoned or were pushed out of the civil rights movement, they also tended to become preoccupied with their own ethnic identity. Jewish veterans of the civil rights struggle often plunged into the campaign for Soviet Jewry, the demanding fight for Israel's survival, the particular agenda of the Jewish people. Resurgent ethnic identity became the new American way, replacing the old, broad civil rights coalitions in which Jews and Blacks had for so long joined hands at the head of the march. Ethnic assertiveness was heard in the land, and the sense of community began to fade away. After civil rights, Vietnam, and Watergate, no one single issue again brought all groups together. Each group went its own way, fighting its own battles; and civil rights, whatever it still is and requires, is no longer a coherent and definable movement.

In this new mood of group separatism, Jews and Blacks have drifted apart. Given the suburban middle-class character of Jewish life, most Jews do not know Blacks on a personal basis. Having a Black maid or employing Hispanic workers may be good things to do, but these are not relationships of equality. Living on opposite sides of the tracks, Jews and Blacks have little human contact and their relationships feed on mutual stereotyping. Blacks see Jews as rich, powerful, and racist; Jews see Blacks as poor, violent, living on welfare, and anti-Semitic.

Aside from the tensions arising from economic inequality, there are other irritants. Some Blacks identify with the Arab cause against Israel, seeing the Palestinians as fellow victims of white oppression. Some Blacks condemn Israel as an ally of the hated regime of South Africa. Because Israel is the symbol of Jewish pride and we see the attitudes of non-Jews as the principal test of their true feelings about Jews, these anti-Israel statements arouse deep distress and anger among American Jews. Some of us see all Blacks as anti-Israel and pro-Arab. The reality is that some Black leaders have been stalwart supporters of Israel and many Blacks still have a positive image of Israel. To most Black people Israel is no more important than Nigeria is to American Jews. We Jews are understandably preoccupied with Israel. Blacks are preoccupied with themselves and with the economic conditions in which 40 percent of their youth in some American cities are out of work, out of school, and out of hope.

Does this mean that Black-Jewish relations are beyond salvaging? There are grounds for hope. Many Blacks and Jews still seem to share a common vision of a just, generous, and open society. Despite our dramatic economic differences, we vote more alike than other racial or religious groups. We both recoil against bigotry; we both wish to see government help solve social inequity; we both support social welfare programs; we both wish to see America extend help to other countries and continue its work toward world peace. In the presidential election of 1976, Jews and Blacks played a major part in the election of Jimmy Carter. These continuing mutual interests should be at least one basis for improved Black-Jewish relations.

Yet any improvement of relations will require Blacks and Jews to change their perception of each other. This generation of Blacks—especially young people—has little awareness of past Jewish contributions to human equality. And even those who are aware want to know: What have you done for me lately? This attitude often infuriates Jews who want to feel some appreciation for sacrifices they often have made to achieve Black rights. Black youths will have to understand recent history, including the Holocaust and its profound impact on the Jewish psyche, if any new relationship is to be forged.

One Black youngster, after viewing the "Holocaust" TV series, said: "My God, I always thought the Holocaust was a Jewish holiday."

And Jews, too, will have to modulate injured feelings and stop expecting constant gratitude. Blacks *today* see Jews more often blocking their hopes for progress than advancing them in busing for integration of schools, in affirmative action, in minority housing, as well as in growing Jewish support for the death penalty, which many Blacks see as code words for "get tough with Blacks."

Increasingly, Jewish attitudes toward Blacks are influenced by the view that Blacks have turned against Jews. The perception of Black anti-Semitism is a powerful barrier to improved relations. Studies indicate that anti-Semitism among Blacks is actually no higher than that among white Christians. While there is a rise in negative attitudes among young Blacks, it is probably no higher than the increase of anti-Black attitudes among Jews. "We moved because the neighborhood was changing," has become a euphemism for "Blacks moved in, so we moved out." Jews frequently associate Blacks with crime, decaying schools and neighborhoods, drugs, and violence.

Jews, in large measure, have lost their empathy for Blacks. They see the results of social disorder, but seldom the causes. Many are more concerned with tranquility shattered than justice denied. Many have little understanding how an inadequate welfare system hurts minority families, how a child can be damaged for life by bad housing and bad schools, how grim the economic picture is for America's twenty-two million Blacks. We want *them* to be sensitive to *our* hurts, but we do not feel an obligation to reciprocate. And neither do they. The result is a drift toward wary competitiveness, punctuated by occasional conflict and even violence.

Can this drift be arrested? It is difficult to foretell at this time, but it's worth a try, because both Jews and Blacks have a common stake in an open and compassionate society. Growth of apartheid in America would threaten both groups. Jews in

South Africa have no safe future in a society of racial arrogance, trembling on the lip of a racial volcano.

We do not have to love each other in order to live with each other. The Nazis, the KKK, the enemies of equality in America —all these are our common enemies. If the lessons of the Holocaust are to have enduring meaning, it means we Jews cannot stand idly by the blood of our brothers and sisters, white or black.

And Blacks, while nourishing their pride and self-worth, must recognize that they cannot change America without allies, just as we Jews have to know that we cannot protect Israel or help Soviet Jews without allies in American life. We have grown edgy and impatient with each other. Bleak silences stretch between us. New bridges must be erected. The demagogues in both groups murmur, why bother? And the enemies of freedom are elated as Jews and Blacks square off against each other, rather than against their true common foes—poverty, ignorance, bigotry, disease, joblessness, and a demeaning welfare system. Whether we like it or not, Blacks and Jews are joined together in a common destiny. It is time to join hands once again.

2

ISRAEL, ZIONISM, THE JEWISH PEOPLE

If we Jews have one commitment which suffers no ambivalence, if we have one bond which unites each and every one of us, it is our profound solidarity with the people and the state of Israel. We may differ about God and religion, politics and education, but on Israel we are solidly united! So why include *Israel* in a book on Jewish *dilemmas*? Why, indeed?

The answer is that Israel is the brilliant mountaintop of our Jewish existence, but deep beneath the surface are embedded the heaviest dilemmas, the most elusive to grasp and the most painful to confront.

CENTRALITY OF ISRAEL FOR THE JEWISH PEOPLE

All but a tiny minority of Jews affirm the validity of the Jewish people and the centrality of Israel in that peoplehood. Clearly, we are a people and our peoplehood transcends our differences. In moments of peril for Israel, as well as in moments of exaltation, we are not Reform, Yiddishist, Zionist, Orthodox, or atheist. We are Jews, a united people, sharing a common destiny, knowing in our bones that what happens to Israel will shape much of our future as Jews. Jewish peoplehood is a powerful force for survival, and that fact is fully appreciated by the American people, the President, the Congress, and the world. Jews can be killed, but "Am Yisrael Chai"—the Jewish people lives!

Is that what is meant by "the centrality of Israel for the Jewish people"? Today, Israel is at the center of Jewish life. But if that means that all of Jewish life throughout the world should be centered on Israel, questions arise. If Israel is central, is the Diaspora secondary or even peripheral? In classic Zionism, every Zionist was obliged to make aliyah to the Jewish homeland, but since the UN's "Zionism equals racism" obscenity, all Jews consider themselves Zionists. In early Zionist theory there was little, if any, future for the Diaspora. At best, it could be a way station to Zion restored. In some ways, the disappearance of the Diaspora was implicit in Zionist ideology, for its essence as a movement was to end Jewish homelessness and to unite the Jewish people with the Jewish land.

Then what does "centrality" mean? Does it mean that American Jewry should subordinate its own needs to the overriding needs of the center, which is the Land of Israel? As a practical matter, we do this gladly in response to the emergency which has continued since 1948. But, should we do it as a matter of principle, even if full peace, for example, came to Israel? Are we saying by "centrality" that the basic future of the Jewish people will be forged in Israel, while in America and elsewhere Jews are doomed to assimilate?

But these are not just questions. There is a haunting dilemma here. For what is the meaning of Israel's centrality if more Israelis go "down" to America than American Jews go "up" on aliyah? What is "centrality" if more Soviet Jews, even while leaving Russia only by virtue of an Israeli visa, choose to live in the United States or Canada or Latin America rather than Israel? These are sad and tragic realities and we deplore them. But what do they say about "centrality"?

But, it is argued on the other side, Israel *is* clearly the spiritual and religious center of the Jewish world, and Jerusalem is the focus of our historic faith and spiritual ideals. But American Jewry rivals Israel in Jewish scholarship, Jewish art, and Jewish learning. Moreover, the "center" is embarrassingly exclusive; the creativity of Reform and Conservative Judaism, so richly expressed in pluralistic America, is denied even elementary recognition in Israel. Orthodoxy in Israel is tainted by its political power and petrified by its iron-clad halachic rigidity. Religion in Israel revolves mostly around rituals and life-cycle events, and rarely faces up to the moral or ethical problems facing Israeli society. Meanwhile, most Israelis live totally secular lives, and many of society's values are shaped by the ever present demands of Israel's military situation and an American-like yearning for supermarket consumer goods.

But, it is said in reply, these are temporary conditions. The "centrality" of Israel lies in its primary place in the consciousness of all Jews everywhere. Do we pray at our Seder tables for the safety of Australian Jews? Do we feel our hearts in our throats when we pick up a newspaper because of our total identification with the Jews of Quebec? Do we mount the barricades and storm the Congress out of concern for South African Jewry? Who can deny the central place in our emotions which Israel commands?

Moreover, what events anywhere else affect us as powerfully as what happens in Israel? When Israel was threatened in 1967, the traumatic memories of the Holocaust were rekindled. When Israel triumphed, we were all ecstatic and every Jew felt ten feet tall. Certainly our self-esteem, our very self-identification, is tied to the fate of Israel. And if Israel were ever destroyed, if the terrorists ever achieved their fondest goal, what then? Could Jewish life elsewhere endure the demoralization of a second Holocaust, the ultimate genocide? This is why Israel is central to the scheme of Jewish peoplehood. Diaspora survival is linked to Israel's survival in the minds of most Jews.

And yet the dilemma persists. Despite all of these questions, are we so sure that Jewish life could not survive even in the face of that unthinkable horror? Despite our terrible history, the Jewish people is indestructible; we have survived Masada as well as Auschwitz; we have survived centuries of Diaspora. And, in any case, there are other equally compelling questions: Could Israel survive if American Jewry somehow were to disappear? Who, then, would provide the economic and political support which is so indispensible to Israel?

There are those who argue that "centrality" is a mere slogan, an empty myth. They contend that we are *equal* partners, not senior or junior, center or marginal. They contend that each of the great Jewries—and especially America and Israel—have crucial roles to play and futures to safeguard. It can even be argued that Judaism as a *living religious civilization* has a better chance of creative fulfillment in America than in Israel. After all, the Jewish community in America is large, affluent, powerful, enjoying the blessings of church-state separation in the freest and wealthiest nation on earth. In America, the synagogue community plays a large role and American Jewry is free to build as vital and powerful and affirming a Jewish life as we have the will to achieve. Here, unlike Israel, a wide spectrum of Jewish religious forms and ideas is encouraged and thrives. We are not limited by external threats to our existence, or the mini-status of the total society. So, why talk of "central"? Israel is part of the Jewish people, not the other way around.

Underlying the argument about "centrality" is the classic Zionist belief that the Diaspora is "galut" (exile). This negation of the exile was an important element of Zionist ideology. In contrast, the American Jewish community is generally optimistic about its present viability and future survival in conditions of democratic freedom. This view is one of "affirmation of the Diaspora." In a recent paper, Dr. Gerson D. Cohen, chancellor of the Jewish Theological Seminary of America (Conservative), challenged the concept of the centrality of Israel, countering with the theme of "the centrality of the Jewish people." He wrote that "Israel will have to send some of its best youth to the Diaspora . . . to study . . . how to be Jews in the modern world."

THE PALESTINIANS

There are other heavy dilemmas too, some dealing with non-Jews in the Jewish state. Modern Zionism was founded by Theodor Herzl in order to end what Herzl saw as the fundamental abnormality of Jewish life—our *homelessness.* Only a homeland, he argued, could reunite the Jewish soul and the Jewish body. Until we had a land of our own, he believed, we would wander across the face of the globe, estranged from our own Jewish selves, subject to persecution at the whim of every ruler in search of a scapegoat. Every people must have a land where it can build its national identity as a matter of right and not at the sufferance of others. Herzl was proved right. The full horror of the Nazi Holocaust revealed that no country in the world really wanted the pitiful Jews who were doomed to destruction by Hitler. Zionism was vindicated by Hitlerism; the Jewish state was born in the ashes of World War II and the destruction of the great historic communities of Europe!

But, ironically, the problem of Jewish homelessness was solved by contributing to the homelessness of another people. Palestine was not an empty place; both Jews and Arabs resided there in uneasy coexistence. Herzl thought that the local Arabs would welcome the coming of a Jewish state and would be won over by the economic benefits generated by a dynamic and modern society. Instead, they rose in angry resistance. Bloody riots killed hundreds of Jews. Pro-Nazi Arab leaders fomented anti-Jewish violence. Ordinary Arabs deeply resented the "invasion" of an alien culture on their soil.

In the War of Independence (1948), almost six hundred thousand Arabs fled their homes in Jaffa, Haifa, and other towns which fell within the borders of the new Jewish state. Arab propaganda claims they were driven out by Jewish aggression; the best evidence is that they fled either in fear of the war or under the orders of Arab rulers who believed the Jews would shortly be massacred and the Arab residents would be able to return in a matter of days and take Jewish property as booty of war.

They have never returned. Kept in refugee camps as political pawns by the Arab states, their children growing up on a propaganda diet of hatred for Israel, the refugees yearned for the day of "return" to their former villages. In their bitterness, more and more joined Arab terrorist groups. The bloody PLO was nurtured in these tawdry camps which are maintained by the UN, principally with the US funds. In the '67 war, Israel occupied the West Bank and Gaza, reuniting Jerusalem, and hundreds of thousands of additional Arabs were uprooted and made homeless.

What should be done about the Palestinians? It is sadly true that nothing was done for the Palestinians when Jordan and Egypt controlled the West Bank and Gaza. They were not even allowed to visit Egypt, much less create a Palestinian state. Under imaginative Israeli Administration, Arabs from the West Bank and Gaza have been accorded the right to cross "open bridges" over the Jordan to visit and to work at relatively good wages in Israel. But year after year, Israeli leaders refused to acknowledge that the Palestinians had become anything more than refugees. "There are no Palestinians," they said. But, increasingly, Palestinian nationalism—no doubt inspired by the success of Zionism—spread among the Palestinians. As one of the most enterprising, best-educated segments of the Arab world, they began to demand their rights *as a people to a national homeland of their own*. Poetry, literature, music, art, and politics converged in a new Palestinian sense of peoplehood—a common cause, a common history, a common destiny.

It is true that the barbarous PLO was annointed by Arab rulers as the "sole representative of the Palestinian people," and no government of Israel could possibly accept the PLO while its charter calls for the liquidation of the Jewish state. It is also true that an increasing number of Palestinians seems willing to settle for a mini-state in the West Bank and Gaza, living side by side with Israel.

Our Jewish dilemma is not less cruel because we avoid its painful challenge: How *should we Jews respond to the Palestinian cry for peoplehood?* Thus far, we have scorned it. We have equated Palestinians and PLO and, since the PLO is anathema, we have avoided the issue. But are the Palestinians a people? If they were not previously, they have now clearly become one. Is it for Jews to decide how a group should define itself? Nothing in Jewish history was more insufferable to us than to have the world define us in *their* terms rather than *ours.* Can Jews—of all peoples—be deaf to the yearning of another people to its claims to national dignity and self-worth?

Of course, it is not all that simple. One Jewish concern is overriding: the *security* of Israel. We fear that, by recognizing the peoplehood of Palestinians, the stage would be set for giving them "legitimate national rights" which would ultimately mean a state with its own flag and identity. If such a state were dominated by and turned into a Soviet-armed staging area by the madmen of the PLO, Israel's very existence would be placed in jeopardy. No Israeli government can be expected to yield to such a suicidal policy.

But the dilemma persists. What is Israel to do with over a million Arabs in the West Bank and Gaza? There are two obvious possibilities. One is to annex these areas. Some Jews say we should do that, calling this area part of a "Greater Israel," promised by God to the Jewish people. This course of action would incense the entire Arab world, making war a likelihood. It would have another undesirable consequence as well, condemning the State of Israel to a zooming Arab birth rate which would, in a matter of decades, swamp Israel's Jewish population, ending for all times the Jewish character of the state. The other alternative is continued occupation of 1½ million alienated and embittered Arabs, certain to grow increasingly hostile to endless foreign control of their destiny. The permanent status of occupiers would also destroy the spiritual and democratic character of Israel, bringing on inevitable abuses of civil liberties and human rights. This, in turn, would isolate Israel further from among even the enlightened nations of the world, including the United States.

Then what are the alternatives? We, in America, cannot determine the political solutions which will safeguard Israel's crucial security needs while accommodating at least the minimal claims of the Palestinian people. Only the government and people of Israel can decide this fateful question.

What is the particular dilemma for us as American Jews? It is to accept the humanity of the Palestinians, to see them as *persons* and as a *people* and not through the prism of anti-Arab stereotypes and slogans. Very few of us truly understand the anguish of the Palestinians. Few, if any, have ever even met a Palestinian. Hardly ever do any Jewish organizations invite a moderate Palestinian to share his or her views with us. To think of all Palestinians as PLO is as sensible as equating all Jews with the Jewish Defense League or the Lubavitcher Chasidim. They, too, are a people of diverse and divergent individuals. But to understand them, we have first to accept them as human beings, with their hopes, their fears, their deepest feelings. Is there any basis for some future relationships between Palestinians and Jews?

Remember, some of the founders of Zionism felt deeply that the ultimate moral test of Zionism was whether or not it could reconcile itself with its Arab neighbors. Have we passed that test? Or can we get off the hook by pointing to unending hostility and aggression from the Arab world? If we fight forever, how long can we keep winning? If the French and Germans could reconcile after two world wars, if Egypt and Israel sign a peace treaty, is it written in the stars that Jews and Palestinians must always be faceless enemies? And what of our Jewish religious tradition which demands that we seek peace and convert enemies to friends? Palestinians, too, are the children of One God. How well will we answer that admonition?

In the present political climate, Palestinians are frequently perceived by the world as "poor, pitiful underdogs" while Israel is seen as the tough, military power in the Middle East. This is a distortion of the first magnitude. But the problem is not resolved by rage or a burning sense of injustice. The dilemma is that we have two peoples with legitimate claims to the same land. Our Jewish history impels us to some sensitivity to other people's feelings of desperation, especially a people with whom we must ultimately come to human terms. How? When? There are no easy answers. But the first, hard step is for both of us to abandon the old slogans which blind us to reality and to each other—and to affirm our common humanity and our common destiny.

A NORMAL STATE FOR A NORMAL PEOPLE?

The question of the Palestinians raises still another dilemma. What *kind* of state is Israel to be? There are those who say that, since Zionism set out to cure the abnormal condition under which the Jewish people had previously lived, the Jewish state need aspire to be no more than a normal state, like any other state in the world. The story is told of how one early Zionist leader expressed satisfaction when he heard that there were now some crooks in the young Jewish state. "See," he said, "we have become a normal state. We have pickpockets and crooks like every other state. *Normal.*"

But there is another view, which springs from the Jewish religious tradition. Israel is to be a *model* state, a *light unto the nations,* a messenger of peace, an example to the civilized world, an expression of God's Covenant with the Jewish people. In this view, Israel is a state, a majority of whose citizens are Jewish, but it is not yet a *Jewish* state.

Which is it to be? Indeed, which *is* it? In many ways, Israel *is* a marvel to the world. No other small state has brought in two million refugees, asking no questions, providing sanctuary to helpless, sick, persecuted, abandoned Jews from Russia, the Arab world, even such medieval places as Yemen. No other small state has displayed the cultural vitality of Israel; more books are published per person than anywhere else in the world. No other small state provided such ambitious and selfless technical assistance to the poor nations of the world —especially Africa—before cynical Arab politics pushed them out. No other small society has tapped the springs of science and technology for the common good as has Israel. No other society, with such limited resources, has made the desert bloom and has built such a sophisticated and humane system of social welfare.

But there is another side to the ledger, too. After three decades, Israel still does not accord full religious liberty to non-Orthodox religious groups, denying Conservative and Reform rabbis the right to officiate at weddings, conversions, funerals, etc. It is grotesque that Israel should extend religious liberty to Christians and Moslems, but not to all Jews. Israel has also failed to bridge the cultural and economic gap between Ashkenazic and Sephardic Jews, even though Israel now has a majority of Jews of Sephardic origin (58 percent). In addition, Israeli Arabs feel themselves to be second-class citizens. Little is done to promote Jewish-Arab harmony on the personal level. Prejudice and antagonism seethe in both communities.

In many ways, the vision of Israel's early chalutzim (pioneers) to create a society of economic equality and social justice has faded under the strains of long periods of austerity and the need to maintain a huge defense burden. As in other countries, a hunger for consumer goods has eclipsed much of the pioneering spirit of the early days and a sense of national purpose seems diminished except in times of a national emergency. In some years, more Israelis leave Israel than are replaced by aliyah. Corruption in business and politics is not uncommon. The economy suffers from intolerable inflation and recurring strikes illustrate frustration and a smoldering sense of economic injustice in the hearts of many Israelis.

The debate goes on. There are those who say that only when Israel is fully freed from external threats and can enjoy peace will it be able to adequately fulfill its Jewish character. Others, including many Israelis, reject the whole notion that Israel must be better than, or different from, any other state. They attribute such an attitude to a Diaspora mentality, born of an inferiority complex or Jewish self-hatred. Why must we be superJews? In a world of corruption and hypocrisy, why do Jews have to be held—or hold ourselves—to a higher standard of conduct than any other people in the world?

CAN JEWS DISSENT ON ISRAEL?

How this dilemma is resolved also bears on another question: Should Diaspora Jewry have a say about issues that bear upon the quality of life in Israel? Those who answer "No" say that domestic issues are the business of Israelis and not Diaspora Jews, that public criticism of Israel's social policies undermines support for Israel.

Those who answer "Yes" say that Israel is the homeland of the Jewish people, of which we are equal partners, and the character—especially the *moral* character—of the Jewish state is decidedly our concern. And we can help Israel to overcome its domestic challenges only if we speak out frankly and involve ourselves in mobilizing support for solutions. The alternative is to create a falsely idyllic picture of Israel, which leads to an escape from reality rather than the necessary frank wrestling with tough issues which require the urgent attention of all Jews, in Israel and the Diaspora. Also implicit in this dilemma is the conflict between moral ideals and the realities of power. Many thoughtful Israelis today lament the loss of the pioneering and socialist values which brought the state into existence. Too often, they say the word "Zionist" has become a term of derision. For what is a "Zionist" now that the state exists? Is it simply a friend and supporter of Israel? A giver to UJA? Then most Jews are Zionists and so are many Christians, including members of the US Senate. A Zionism which embraces everybody is no movement at all. Has Zionism, as the cultural and spiritual liberation movement of the Jewish people, become outdated once the State has come into being? Many people think so; many others, however, believe that Zionism must now be redefined and revitalized to respond to the new situation. The leaders of Reform and Conservative Judaism obviously believe the latter because these religious movements have now joined the World Zionist Organization alongside Orthodox Judaism and every other segment of Jewish life. Reform has created its own Zionist movement (ARZA).

In the press of the practical tasks of nation building and the constant search for peace, the memory of what early Zionism really was, in all its cultural and spiritual ideals, tends to fade from the minds of Israelis and Jews of the Diaspora.

This original Zionism was both revolutionary and idealistic —one of the great liberation forces of history. One of the main streams of early Zionist thought was a visionary commitment to the reality that Palestine was not vacant and that Jews had to forge a human and political relationship with the existing Arab people. This ideal stemmed from the deepest ethical motives and traditions of the Jewish people.

Advocates of this early Zionism were among the most respected names in the Jewish history of recent generations. Foremost among them was Ahad Ha-Am, writer and philosopher of the "Return to Zion." One of his disciples was Rabbi Judah L. Magnes, a Reform rabbi who made aliyah in 1922 and became the founder of the Hebrew University which he served as president until his death in 1946.

Ahad Ha-Am, a Russian Jewish thinker of the highest order, was a "cultural Zionist." He taught that a Jewish homeland must be reconciled with "consideration for the national rights of the Palestinian Arabs." He rejected the conventional wisdom of other Zionist leaders who insisted that the Balfour Declaration was a mandate for a Jewish state in all of Palestine. Ahad Ha-Am stressed what others chose to ignore—that the British pledge in the Balfour Declaration was conditioned by the clause "that nothing shall be done which may prejudice the civil and religious rights of existing non-Jewish communities in Palestine." He was haunted by the moral compulsion that the development of a Jewish homeland should not displace or degrade those Arabs who also have "a genuine right to the land due to generations of residence and work upon it." To him, Palestine was a "common possession of two peoples."

Following Ahad Ha-Am's death, Magnes carried on the unpopular struggle, bringing Arabs and Jews together to work for a binational state in which the rights of both would be protected by constitutional safeguards with two official languages. "One of the greatest cultural duties of the Jewish people," he said, "is the attempt to enter the Promised Land, not by means of conquest as Joshua, but through peaceful and cultural means, through hard work, sacrifice, love, and with a decision not to do anything which cannot be justified before the world conscience."

Another of the early pioneers, A.D. Gordon, shared some of these ideals. His principal thesis was that the Jewish people's rebirth would come primarily from building a homeland with its own hands. He was the advocate of the dignity of labor and he practiced what he preached, working as a manual laborer in the fields and vineyards of Palestine. Gordon was a secular mystic who combined nationalism with a universal messianism. "We were the first to proclaim," he wrote, "that man is created in the image of God. We must go further and say: the *nation* must be created in the image of God. Not because we are better than others, but because we have borne upon our shoulders and suffered all which calls for this. It is by paying the price of torments the like of which the world has never known that we have won the right to be the first in this world of Creation." He died long before the dark night of the Holocaust and the gleaming dawn of Israel's reemergence into history.

To Gordon, the ultimate test of Jewish integrity would be our treatment of the Arabs. "Our attitude toward them," he wrote, "must be one of humanity, of moral courage which remains on its highest plane, even if the behavior of the other side is not all that is desired. Indeed, their hostility is all the more reason for our humanity." He believed that "we must aim at the correct relationships to man and the nations in general and to the Arabs in particular."

The illustrious religious teacher, Martin Buber, also believed that the moral challenge to Zionism was its willingness to share the land between two peoples. He pleaded for the "harnessing of nationalistic impulses and a solution based on compromise between two peoples."

All of these were lonely voices in the wilderness. They were like the prophets of old, idealistic and "unrealistic." They would no doubt weep in despair if they had lived to see the seemingly endless tragedy of Arab-Jewish hostility, wars, and hatred over the past decades. They would have been cheered by the historic breakthrough of peace between Egypt and Israel in 1979.

Could the past thirty years have been otherwise? Perhaps not. The Holocaust generated so fierce a sense of desperation that there was little energy left to indulge the yearnings of the early Zionists. Nor did unrelenting Arab hostility and bloody riots fomented by pro-Nazi Arab leaders predispose Jews to consider such idealistic notions as a binational state. The urgent need to establish the Jewish state—and its survival against formidable dangers—swamped all other considerations. It probably could not have been otherwise. Is it not the case that the power of moral ideals always must give way to the necessities of power? It is one thing for A.D. Gordon to spin his dreams of humanity in the vineyards of Petach Tikvah; it is quite another thing for a Ben-Gurion to have to hold the state together against overpowering pressures from without and within. Framing a vision and running a state are two different realms of reality.

But is there no connection whatever between ideals and reality? Can Israel fulfill its true potential if there is no link to its prophetic heritage? The present truth is one at which no realist should blink. Jews and Arabs of Israel, fellow citizens, have little social and human contact. The reverence for the dignity of labor, which Gordon celebrated, has been turned upside down;

it is Arab workers who frequently do the sweat work in Israel, even on some kibbutzim. Arabs and Jews see each other across a chasm of stereotypes and it takes a miracle like Sadat's visit to Jerusalem to break the "psychological impasse" so that Jews and Arabs can glimpse each other's humanity. The Arab contributions to this sorry state of affairs are a matter of dismal record, but have we Jews—in Israel and the Diaspora—done all that we could have done to generate decent human relations between Arabs and Jews?

The dreamers of early Zionism are gone. But has the dream altogether died with them? Is there any chance for the survival of a Jewish state in the midst of a vast Arab area? In the end, coexistence may be the only hope for any future existence and the visions of Buber, Ahad Ha-Am, Magnes, and Gordon may yet prove their value in a world of tough militarian and hard-nosed power politics. This particular dilemma goes deep into the Jewish past and the sources of our moral inspiration. In many ways, it will shape the nature of our Jewish future.

CAN JEWS DISSENT ON ISRAEL'S POLICIES?

One more difficult dilemma arises from the question: What do we, as American Jews, do when we seriously differ with certain policies pursued by the government of Israel? This is not quite so easy an issue as one might first think, because what American Jews say publicly frequently translates into large public opinion in the United States and sometimes even into the policies followed by our government. The United States of America and America's Jews are Israel's most powerful and important allies and their words and action have a direct and crucial impact on the well-being and security of the Jewish state. So, how should we act when our viewpoints and convictions differ in matters of great importance? The question is best illustrated by the case of an organization called Breira, formed in the early 1970s by a small group of Jews in the US who banded together to advance alternative proposals for peace in the Middle East. Many observers found their ideas ill-advised and wrongheaded. But the reaction to Breira was, for the most part, not one of legitimate controversy about their ideas; it was a strident attack on their personal integrity, their motivations, their Jewish loyalty, and their right to criticize Israel's policies publicly. The attack worked; it virtually destroyed the group. It was a sorry example of Jewish McCarthyism in action.

The sorry end of Breira sharpens the issue of how American Jews can express public disagreement with the policies of the government of Israel. On their part, Jews in Israel vigorously debate, argue, and dissent on every major issue of Israeli policy. Should US Jews be silent partners or—worse —predictable amen-sayers or messenger carriers for the particular policy of whatever leadership is in power in Israel? One can say "No" to that question and still argue that Israelis earn the right to dissent because they—and not we in America—have to fight and die for miscalculation of policy. Many American Jews were zealous and outspoken in opposition to their own government on Vietnam and Watergate, disagreeing with those who demanded: "My country right or wrong." Are we to be dissenters in America and silent spectators about events in Israel when our conscience tells us that something is wrong?

American Jewry has not yet clarified its proper role in relation to policies of the State of Israel. To say we have no right to speak is to condemn ourselves to second-class status within the Jewish people, to do a disservice to Israel in assessing the impact of its policies, and to violate our own beliefs and perhaps conscience. Can anyone honestly deny our right to demand full religious liberty for Reform and Conservative Jews in Israel?

But the other side of the coin is that speaking out for our rights in Israel is quite a different matter from speaking out on matters of security and foreign policy for which Israelis—and not we—must pay the ultimate price. Moreover, Jewish voices of dissent are indeed used by Israel's enemies and are trumpeted by the media to undermine Israel's position. Those are grave considerations and they must weigh on every friend of Israel and every Jew committed to the Jewish people.

But even this does not resolve the matter. If I am committed to Israel, am I automatically committed to Begin or Peres or Weizmann or whoever is in power and am I expected to defend every policy enunciated by that government, even if I believe it is disastrous for Israel, ruinous to American public opinion and perhaps even morally wrong? It is often said that if American Jews feel compelled to dissent, we should do so directly and privately with Israel's leadership. This may be good judgment in most cases. But what if they spurn our advice? Or what if—as in the question of the rights of Palestinian Arabs—the controversy rises to an issue of profound moral and ethical principle? If we suppress our fears and doubts and silence our conscience, may we not be doing greater harm to Israel and to ourselves than the harm of showing divisions in our midst?

Every thoughtful American Jew will face this dilemma at one time or another. If one speaks out, one may risk attacks on one's Jewish loyalty and even one's integrity. But a Jewish community sensitive to civil liberties must learn to respect dissent and divergent views within the Jewish community as much as it safeguards civil liberties in America as a whole. Democracy, like charity, begins at home. And failure to resolve this dilemma could be fatal for the Jewish people and for Israel itself.

3

CIVIL LIBERTIES

FREE SPEECH

Skokie, Illinois, is a suburb of Chicago. It has a population of approximately 60,000 persons. Some 40,000 Jews live in the town; 7,000 are survivors of Nazi concentration camps, an extraordinary proportion. To America —and perhaps much of the world—Skokie is remembered as the place where the American Nazi party sought to organize a march in 1978 "to combat Jewish control of America." City officials refused to grant a license for such a demonstration. The Nazis went to court, asserting their First Amendment rights had been violated and that they had the right to march in Nazi uniform to express their ideas, however unpopular.

The American Civil Liberties Union went to court to support the right of the Nazis to march. Leaders of the Jewish Defense League announced that, whatever the courts held, that group would not permit the Nazis to march. Finally, as the danger of confrontation reached a fever pitch, the march was switched from Skokie to Marquette Park in Chicago and passed with only minor disturbances. The DILEMMAS of Skokie, however, have lost none of their acute relevance, as the following correspondence will show.

Dear Rabbi:

I am writing this letter at 3:00 A.M., Saturday morning, because your sermon last evening on "Why I must resign from the American Civil Liberties Union" has agitated and upset me so badly that I realized I could never get to sleep unless I share my reactions with you while they are still red-hot. I have always respected you and your views so greatly that I was almost in awe of you. That respect, of course, is unimpaired and I trust you will not let this honest difference affect our valued friendship of many years standing. But, regardless, I am terribly disappointed and distressed by your sermon on this Shabbat and I have to get it off my chest.

Your sermon is a prime example of what has been described as a backlash of "further withdrawal of the American Jewish community from social action and into a posture of self-defense." Your attempt to find a "clear and present danger" whenever "mental and emotional injury" results from free speech is a most serious threat to the First Amendment.

You compare defending the right of Nazis to march in Skokie, Illinois, with defending "the Nazis at the Nuremberg trial." At Nuremberg, Nazis were tried for heinous crimes, including the slaughter of 6 million Jews. The Nazis in Skokie propose to express ideas—horrible and odious as they are. The distinction between *advocacy* of genocide and the *act* of genocide goes to the essence of the First Amendment and the American experience in which Jews have been among the prime beneficiaries.

Throughout European history, Jews, as a minority, have "offended" majorities which have used laws and government to keep Jews from inflicting "mental and emotional injury" upon Christian sensibilities. Of all people, Jews should understand the danger in using government to suppress minority views —whether political or religious. Blacks marching in Selma disturbed the emotional and mental health of Southern white bigots who saw their society crumbling. The First Amendment protects the speaker, not the offended sensibilities of the audience. "Mental and emotional injury" is the price we must pay for a free society. That, after all, is the essence of the First Amendment which provides that:

"Congress shall make no law respecting an establishment of religion, or prohibiting the free exercise thereof; or abridging the freedom of speech, or of the press; or the right of the people peaceably to assemble, and to petition the government for a redress of grieveance."

Unlike the Jewish Defense League, which takes the law into its own hands by threatening violence to Nazis, you want to use government to censor speech and assembly.

The American system believes that falsehood when exposed to the marketplace of ideas will be rejected. When we can no longer trust this system, then Jews will have most to lose. Because Jews have historically realized the special significance of protecting free speech for all, ACLU has always been supported very significantly by Jews and Jews are prominent in ACLU's leadership. Presently its executive director is a Jew—a refugee from Nazi Germany. ACLU's national chairman is Jewish and a large proportion of its national Board of Directors is Jewish. In its defense of free speech for Nazis in Skokie and the KKK in Mississippi, the board remains steadfast in its defense of ACLU's position in this matter.

It is understandable that Jews have the strongest abhorrence of Nazis and the doctrines which they preach. It is more important to Jews, however, that America remain strong in its defense of the First Amendment. Rather than quit ACLU in protest, Jews should more than ever rally around the organization which does more than any other to protect minority rights. Jews should be the last to abandon ACLU, for when there is no longer an ACLU, America will not be a safe place for Jews.

Paul

Dear Paul:

I have read your letter. While I disagree profoundly, I am truly grateful to you for taking our relationship seriously enough to challenge my ideas. The pulpit must be a dialogue, not a monologue, and you are right to debate me when you think I'm off base.

Jews have been receiving concerned advice from friendly non-Jewish and Jewish sources not to abandon the American Civil Liberties Union. This advice is occasioned by the ACLU's defense of the Nazi party and by the consequent flood of resignations from the ACLU. Right off, I want to declare my belief that those who, like you, defend the ACLU position generally do so out of devotion to the principles of the First Amendment and out of profound concern for the Jewish people. . . .

Many years ago I resigned from the ACLU when a similar Nazi problem had arisen in the community. Since then I have attempted to think through a position which could do justice to the Bill of Rights and to the inalienable rights of Jews. In the first place, the ACLU and its supporters would have a difficult time making a case for Jews contributing their resources for the right of Nazis to promote Jewish destruction. Leaving aside for the moment the ACLU's right to defend the Nazis, does it have a moral right to protest the refusal of Jews to support the ACLU position? Even the most devoted civil libertarian cannot make a reasonable claim that the victim has an obligation to come to the aid of his agressor.

The ACLU would respond that membership in that organization is for the support of a principle, not persons, and that it handles many other cases. My response is that this case is the most notorious and indefensible that the ACLU has taken on, that in this case the ACLU cannot separate itself from the Nazi cause. Therefore, on this issue alone, I not only applaud the massive resignation by Jews . . . but, as long as it persists in its present course, I could not fault its remaining Jewish members if they were to quit out of self-respect.

As to the Jewish lawyers in the ACLU, the principle is the same. I asked a Jewish friend who supported the ACLU position if he, as a lawyer, would have defended the Nazis at the Nuremberg trial. His long pause persuaded me that he got the point. Every conscientious person who entertains deep convictions knows that there are moral borders at which he may have to disqualify himself.

What the ACLU is doing in this particular case is to jeopardize freedom in America, not to enhance it. Its supporters argue that, if any group is restrained from demonstrating, then all groups are in danger of similar restraint.

On the contrary, I contend that Nazis use the democratic process not to establish the principle of freedom but to undermine it. If this tactic can be successfully employed, then the Bill of Rights could conceivably be subverted by those who use it as a shield. . . . Where free institutions are made a mockery of by those who would destroy them, the credibility and effectiveness of those institutions become seriously impaired.

That is why the Jewish community under the guidance of a distinguished legal team is making a significant contribution to American thought. It is attempting to establish a position between the denial of rights and the abuse of rights by raising the issue of mental and emotional injury when devotees of genocide insist on abusive confrontation. . . . The failure to distinguish between the claims of virtually all dissenters and the claims of those who are bent on genocide represents a clear and present danger for freedom in America.

Yours,
Rabbi

The dreadful dilemma debated above cuts to the bone of Jewish life in America today. Skokie was only the symbol of a deep-seated conflict of values seething beneath the surface of Jewish life. How really secure are we Jews? Can we rely for our safety on the abstractions of constitutional safeguards? Have we become so much a part of an obsolete liberalism that we have bartered away our own Jewish interests in the name of universalism? Or, have we Jews become so panicky about mere nuisances that we jeopardize long-term interests for short-term gains? Has the Jewish community abandoned its faith in civil liberties now that the issue has come home for us, just as many Jews gave up on racial integration when it came to OUR schools and neighborhoods?

American Jews have been among the firmest supporters of civil liberties in American life. A substantial proportion of the membership of the ACLU was Jewish, although at least 4,000 Jews cancelled their membership over the Skokie controversy. During the dark reign of Senator Joseph McCarthy, when free speech was chilled by loose charges of communism and treason, Jews overwhelmingly opposed McCarthy, despite the fact that the senator was not anti-Semitic and was aided by two Jewish lawyers. Even when the demagogic senator was winning approval of a majority of Americans, Jewish organizations and many Jewish individuals fought vigorously against the blight of fear and conformity he fomented. Finally, American common sense was restored, and one of the blackest eras in American life came to an end.

Then in the seventies came the firestorm of Watergate. It came as a severe shock to Americans that President Nixon participated in a cover-up of a criminal conspiracy to protect a political intelligence operation against investigation by Congress and the reach of the law. We know that the FBI and the CIA violated the rights of American citizens by wiretapping, opening of mail, and by maintaining millions of illegal dossiers on those who legally protested against the Vietnam War or racial injustice. These agencies broke into premises, bugged the phones of reporters, as well as the offices of legitimate organizations, provoked violent incidents to discredit dissenting groups, and plotted to destroy the reputations of such civil rights leaders as Martin Luther King. In short, arms of the government of the United States sought to stifle the exercise of dissenting opinion with the covert support of the President.

We have not yet made fully certain that the intelligence community will be a servant—and not the master—of the citizenry, although the President and the Congress have since taken action to place these agencies under democratic check. But no one should ever again assume that the Constitution is a self-enforcing document and that our liberties cannot be tampered with. Richard Nixon misused power, obstructed justice, and thought he was above the law. But other presidents besides Nixon also took short cuts on due process in times of stress, and the only sure guarantee of our liberties is an alert and vigilant American press and public, unafraid to defend our fundamental right to think, say, and write what we believe, regardless of who likes it or does not like it.

Our Jewish tradition teaches us "never put your trust in princes," and that is good advice, whether our leaders are Republicans or Democrats, liberals or conservatives. We, the people, are the masters and our elected servants must serve us and our liberties. Most Jews continue to cherish the traditions of civil liberties and respond strongly to pressures against these liberties.

A letter from the American Civil Liberties Union:

Dear Friend:

I have received a number of letters critical of the ACLU's defense of free speech for Nazis and I will try to respond to the arguments that appear most frequently.

One comment is that, if the Nazis come to power, the ACLU and its leaders would not be allowed to survive. Of course, that is true. Civil liberties is the antithesis of Nazism.

Perhaps that explains best why we defend free speech for Nazis. We don't share their values. We don't take guidance from them. We defend free speech for Nazis—or anyone else—because we say that government may not put any person or group beyond the pale of constitutional protection.

The Constitution is absolute in its language. It allows "no law . . . abridging the freedom of speech, or of the press. . . ." No law means no law. It does not mean giving government officials some leeway to pick out groups that are so despicable that they should be denied freedom of speech.

Some of the people who write to us about Skokie point out that free speech does not protect the right of a person falsely to shout fire in a crowded theater. Quite right. When a person shouts fire in a theater, no one else has an opportunity to express a contrary view before a panic ensues. Free speech can't operate. That is what the courts call a "clear and present danger."

Suppose a Nazi speaker, in front of a mob of sympathizers, said: "There's a Jew. Let's get him." If the Nazi refrained from participating directly in any resulting violence, he still would not have any valid defense of free speech. As in the example of shouting fire in a crowded theater, the violence would follow before anyone could present an opposing view. Free speech could not operate.

Skokie is altogether different. It has a large Jewish community and is very hostile to the Nazis. If a Nazi marching in Skokie should call for violence against Jews, it won't take place. The only likelihood of violence in Skokie is on the part of listeners to the Nazis who become so enraged at the message of the Nazis that they attack the Nazis.

But listener rage against a speaker can never be the basis for banning speech. If that were allowed, Martin Luther King, Jr. could never have marched in Selma, anti-war demonstrators could never have marched on or near a military base, the Jewish Defense League could never have picketed the Russian embassy, and anti-Nixon demonstrators could never have picketed the White House.

Some letter writers say that group defamation should not be permitted. The late Edmond Cahn dealt with this subject in a notable address delivered at the Hebrew University in Jerusalem in 1962. If there were a prohibition against group defamation, said Cahn:

"The officials could begin by prosecuting anyone who distributed the Christian Gospels, because they contain many defamatory statements not only about Jews but also about Christians; they show Christians failing Jesus in his hour of deepest tragedy. Then the officials could ban Greek literature for calling the rest of the world 'barbarians.'

"And there are many more examples one could cite. Literally

applied, a group-libel law would leave our bookshelves empty and us without desire to fill them."

Some letter writers invoke the memory of Germany between 1919 and 1933. To anyone familiar with that period, the notion that it died of an excess of civil liberty is the wildest nonsense. On the contrary, the Weimar Republic was incapable of protecting civil liberty. Free speech did not exist in Weimar Germany because the government would not safeguard it.

Some letter writers complain that the ACLU should use its limited resources elsewhere. If we wanted to duck the issue, we could have said something along those lines. But it would have been false. The ACLU takes all cases in which we believe free speech is at stake. The ACLU has always defended free speech for Nazis, the KKK, or anyone else. We will only deserve to call ourselves a civil liberties organization so long as we continue to insist that everyone is entitled to freedom of speech.

The Nazis may despise us—and we certainly despise them—but we intend to continue to be governed by our rules and free speech for those we despise and those who despise us.

Thank you for writing. I am grateful for the letters I have received, many of them written with the vigor characteristic of a people accustomed to exercising freedom of speech.

Sincerely,
Aryeh Neier, [former] Executive Director

HOLOCAUST SURVIVORS: A VULNERABLE GROUP

By Stephen Fuchs, rabbi of Temple Isaiah, Columbia, MD.

Jewish law accords the victims of great suffering—the widowed and the orphaned—an extraordinary degree of compassion and protection. The Torah reflects their special status: "You shall not mistreat a widow or a fatherless child. If you afflict them in any way, I shall surely heed them when they cry out to me." (Exodus 22:21–22)

Abraham Ibn Ezra commented that, even if only one individual added to the suffering of widows and orphans, the entire community incurred divine wrath if it did not rise up to protect the victims.

When the Hebrew Bible and later Jewish tradition speak of the widow and the orphan, they speak broadly of particularly vulnerable individuals whose prior suffering demands that protection.

Many people who experienced the Holocaust are still alive. They have lost their families; many have lost their mobility, their sexuality, and their ability to hope that life can be good and positive because of the horror they lived through in Europe a generation ago.

Those survivors are a unique group of people whose immeasurable suffering entwines itself into any discussion of free speech as it applies to the rights of Nazis to march in full regalia and thereby evoke memories of Hitler's policies and practices.

It is true, as the *Washington Post* noted recently, that the Supreme Court has followed a zigzag path in applying the First Amendment's guarantee of freedom of speech. It is not true, as the editorial contended, that such a zigzag path is unfortunate.

Freedoms are rarely absolute. Often one conflicts with another. When such clashes occur, courts must decide which freedom should take precedence.

As Felix Frankfurter wrote in his opinion in *Dennis* v. *United States* in 1951: "Not every type of speech occupies the same position on the scale of values. There is no substantial public interest in permitting certain kinds of utterances . . . those which by their very utterance inflict injury or tend to incite an immediate breach of the peace."

In arguing for the primacy of free speech, the *Washington Post* editorial quoted Oliver Wendell Holmes's famous statement: "If there is any principle of the Constitution that more imperatively calls for attachment than any other it is the principle of free thought—not free thought for those who agree with us but freedom for the thought that we hate."

The argument there is not with hateful thoughts but with the immediate consequences wrought by the public expression of certain hateful thoughts. An equally famous quote from Justice Holmes's 1919 opinion in *Schenk* v. *United States* speaks to that vital issue. He wrote: "The most stringent protection of free speech would not protect a man in falsely shouting fire in a theater and causing a panic. It does not even protect a man from an injunction against uttering words that may have all the effect of force."

The justices differ over the magnitude a potential disaster must possess to permit that disaster to restrict free speech. However, the Nazi issue pits basic values of the American system against one another and forces us to confront our priorities.

When in April the American Nazi party opened the Rudolph Hess Bookstore in San Francisco directly across from Congregation B'nai Emunah, a huge swastika stared defiantly at the synagogue attended largely by refugees of Hitler's Holocaust. Sixty percent of B'nai Emunah's members are concentration-camp survivors.

The question is: Which takes precedence—the Nazis' right of free speech or the emotional sensibilities and, yes, the physical well-being of this unique group of Americans?

The story of Tauba Weiss, which appeared in the *San Francisco Examiner,* is unfortunately not an uncommon one among Holocaust refugees.

She sobbed: " 'I lost four brothers and two sisters. I saw them take my mother away.'

"She knelt and put her hands to her neck and described how as a boy her husband watched the Nazis 'chop his father' to death.

" 'So,' she said through high-pitched cries, 'if you see a swastika you get all hysterical.' "

Tauba Weiss's fears are hardly unique. Similar reactions are stirred in thousands of Americans by the sight of a Nazi uniform or the sound of exhortations similar to those that preceded the destruction of one-third of the world's Jews a generation ago.

The reflex of many of these people is instant and unavoidable. Public Nazi demonstrations involve a clear and present danger to the physical and emotional health of these citizens.

The fact that we have, as Aryeh Neier of the American Civil Liberties Union wrote in a recent *Washington Post* article, "the freedom to express with all due vehemence our detestation for the Nazis" does nothing to help the already scarred Holocaust victim. If the Nazis were only "enemies of freedom" with evil intent, there would be insufficient reason to stifle them. Unlike any of Neier's other examples, though, a Nazi march and rally would bring severe and immediate suffering on a significant group of Americans.

No, the survival of the country is not imminently threatened by allowing Nazis to parade, but the health and welfare of certain Americans clearly are. Far more is involved than the mere freedom to be vile.

The courageous "widows and orphans" of humanity's greatest tragedy deserve a special measure of protection. Lest our society merit the divine wrath of which Ibn Ezra spoke, we must rise up as one body to prevent their further suffering.

CENSORSHIP

Similarly, in local communities, Jews are usually found among the opponents of censorship. Blatant censorship is not as common as it once was, but neither is it extinct. In 1978, the Island Trees Board of Education in Long Island, New York, ordered the removal of nine books from the high school library. These books included Bernard Malamud's Pulitzer prize-winning novel, *The Fixer, Slaughterhouse Five* by Kurt Vonnegut, *Soul on Ice* by Eldridge Cleaver, *The Naked Ape* by Desmond Morris, *Down These Mean Streets* by Piri Thomas, and *Best Short Stories by Negro Writers,* edited by Langston Hughes. Inspired by an ultra-conservative group called Parents of New York United, the school board decided these books were "anti-American" and that most residents of the area did not want them in their schools. A few years earlier, in Kanawha County (West Virginia), protests against the use of books (including Cleaver's *Soul on Ice*) that were deemed to be "atheist, un-Christian, and Communist" turned violent. An elementary school was bombed, autos were blown up, and school board members were physically attacked.

Jewish groups opposed these efforts at censorship, regarding them as gross violations of the Constitutional safeguards of civil liberties. Even campaigns against pornographic literature leave many Jews uneasy because of the difficulty of definition and the danger of censoring the good along with the bad. We have seen that many Jews become impatient with civil libertarian considerations when the Jewish community itself seems threatened, but in general they tend to lean toward untrammeled freedom, believing that the risks of freedom are smaller than the risks of suppression, book-burning, and censorship. The security of Jews is best protected by the maintenance of American liberties for every American, however odious the ideas involved. This means freedom for atheists, communists, anarchists, and anyone else with unpopular ideas. The line must be drawn at deeds, not words.

Why have Jews inclined so markedly toward civil liberties? In the Jewish value system, learning is a priority. Ignorance is regarded as virtually the ultimate sin. Even in the shabby medieval ghettoes of Europe, where Jews suffered severe physical and social disabilities, Jewish learning was an oasis in a desert of gentile illiteracy. Jews, as the People of the Book, have maintained a profound reverence for study, for literature, and for the life of the mind.

Jewish tradition cherishes free speech. "These and those may be the words of the Living God," said the rabbis, insisting on respect for honest differences of opinion. The assertion of unpopular opinions illumines the Bible. The prophet Nathan denouncing King David for having stolen Bathsheba from her husband; Elijah acusing King Ahab for his evildoings; Job talking back to God; Abraham arguing with God—these are but a few of the many examples of fiercely unpopular opinions freely and openly expressed. The Talmud is an ocean of opinions, majority and minority, each accorded the honor of inclusion in the Sacred Writings. The schools of Hillel and Shammai differed sharply in most of their interpretations of the law and the Talmud included positions of both—and in detail. Studies of the shtetl—small Jewish towns in Eastern Europe —confirm the respect for differing views which animated these tightly-knit Jewish communities. This regard for free expression, this sensitive respect for differences has, without any doubt, left its mark upon Jews of our age. In a sense, Jews were against McCarthyism thousands of years before Joseph McCarthy.

This is not to pretend that Jewish history could be certified 100 percent libertarian by the ACLU. Jeremiah was sentenced to die as a traitor; Amos was denounced; Elisha ben Abuyah was thrown out of the Sanhedrin for heresy; Spinoza was excommunicated; and the Orthodox rabbinate in modern Israel is no friend of civil liberties. But these—and many others—are aberrations from the mainstream of Jewish tradition which enshrines the free mind.

PRIVACY

Judaism not only affirms our right to speak our conscience; it also affirms our essential right to privacy. We live today in a time of mounting invasions of personal privacy and the growing use of wiretaps, electronic bugging, and interminable snooping by law-enforcement agencies. The potential threat which the new technology of surveillance poses to the dignity and privacy of the individual has been the subject of a number of studies. Unless the American public remains alert to the assaults on its privacy, it is possible that the oft-proposed National Data Center will one day be a fact of American life. Such a computerized data bank would store all the vital information on all citizens of the country. What such a monster would ultimately portend for privacy and liberty can only be imagined.

The late Supreme Court Justice William O. Douglas warned that personal privacy "has almost vanished in the United States." He added that Americans "may in time rebel against its loss." Pointing out that "practically nothing is now immune from search or seizure," Justice Douglas asserted that "only rebellion, I think, can save us from ultimate suffocation."

Jewish teachings anticipated many of the problems incorporated in the Fourth Amendment to the Constitution: "The rights of the people to be secure in their persons, houses, papers, and effects against unreasonable searches and seizures shall not be violated and no warrants shall issue but upon probable cause, supported by oath or affirmation, and particularly describing the place to be searched, and the person or things to be seized."

Surprisingly enough, Jewish law went further than the Fourth Amendment in securing a person's right to privacy, best illustrated by this biblical passage: "When you make your neighbor any manner of loan, you shall not go into his house to fetch his pledge. You shall stand outside, and the man to whom you made the loan shall bring the pledge to you." Even non-physical invasion of privacy was forbidden by Jewish teaching. The Mishnah prohibited the installation of windows facing the courtyard of a neighbor. Each family had the right to be free of even neighborly snooping. Similarly, if a family's roof happened to be adjacent to a neighbor's courtyard, the owner of the roof was obliged to constuct a visual barrier to prevent violation of the neighbor's privacy. These were not merely moral obligations. They were legal responsibilities enforceable by courts.

Eavesdropping, gossip-mongering, and slander are strongly condemned in Jewish teaching. "Let your neighbor's honor be as dear to you as your own." Talmud tells the story that a distinguished teacher, Rabbi Ami, expelled a scholar from the academy because he disclosed a report he had received confidentially 22 years earlier. Unauthorized disclosure was strictly prohibited, and the privacy of mail was absolutely safeguarded.

Living in the present, we seem to be as eager to bare our souls as to have others bare theirs for us; it is chastening to recall that halachah, Jewish law, bade the Jew, as a moral duty, to protect one's own privacy as well as that of one's neighbor. Privacy was seen as an aspect of one's sanctity as a child of God. Privacy is a shield to human personality. Without it, one is stripped of individuality and selfhood. Deprived of privacy, a person is dehumanized. Jewish sensitivity to civil liberties—and to the precious right to be left alone—has much relevance to our current struggle to resist the onslaught of brainwashing, subliminal advertising, bugging, wiretapping, and other technological intrusions.

YOU CAN MAKE A DIFFERENCE

An individual, by taking a stand, can make a difference in the ongoing battle for freedom and civil liberties. Sometimes that difference can be unexpectedly large and lasting. Here is an example:

In the winter of 1975, when the Jewish world was reeling from the shock of a UN resolution equating Zionism with racism, protests and demonstrations were mounted everywhere. In Dallas, 2,000 delegates to the General Assembly of the UAHC, led by the youth delegation of the NFTY, joined in moving song and prayer against this international anti-Semitic obscenity. Similarly, in thousands of local communities, Jews called upon their Christian neighbors to rally with them to protest this indignity.

In one California town—San Jose—Jewish youngsters from the Reform Temple Emanu-El gathered at the local shopping center to seek signatures on a petition opposing the UN resolution. Leading the temple youth were Michael Robins, son of Rabbi and Mrs. David Robins of Temple Emanu-El, and David Marcus, son of Fred Marcus, educator at the temple.

Both boys had been active in CAFTY (California Federation of Temple Youth) at Camp Swig (Saratoga, CA), as well as in their local youth group.

The managers of the shopping center (Prune Yard) came out and demanded that the petitioners leave the shopping center because they were "trespassing on private property." Michael and David refused, contending that they had a right to reach the public and that a petition is a fundamental expression of free speech. The boys were outraged by what they regarded as a denial of their civil rights. They shared their concern with their families and others in the congregation.

An attorney, who was past president of the temple (Philip Hammer), agreed to take their case without charge and they went to court to assert the right of free speech inside privately owned shopping centers. Because of the serious threat to their property rights, as they conceived this case to be, shopping centers set aside substantial sums to fight the case— expending in excess of $250,000 before the US Supreme Court finally resolved the case.

Step by step, Mike and David pushed their case through the legal system, losing in the Superior Court, appealing to the next higher court. Finally, after five years, the US Supreme Court, in June of 1980, handed down a landmark decision in the case, which will be known to legal history as *Prune Yard Shopping Center v. Robins et al.* By unanimous decision, the highest court upheld the right of Michael and David—and, therefore, all citizens—to freedom of speech and assembly even in a privately owned shopping center. Michael and David (who was the *et al* referred to in the historic decision) had, by their persistence, struck a blow not only for their own rights; they had enlarged the definition of civil liberties for all Americans.

When the Supreme Court acted, Mike was already a sophomore at Reed College, while David was a sophomore at the University of California at Santa Cruz. They were elated. "Some people thought it was an absurd attempt," said Mike. "They didn't think we could take on big business and win. But in this case the democratic process worked—financial resources were not an issue." Added Dave: "It proves that the individual can still make a difference. Two people can still make their mark on society." David went out to celebrate by having lunch with his father who had come to America to escape Nazi persecution two generations ago. Fred Marcus had taught David that free speech must never take a back seat and is always worth fighting for.

4

THE JEWISH FAMILY IN TRANSITION

Ask what one value is most characteristic of Jewish life and the answer—from Jew and non-Jew alike—will be good family life. Indeed, some historians believe that the concept of wholesome family life, derived from Jewish tradition, may well be the crowning gift which Jews gave to world civilization. Implied in this valuation are warmth, closeness, mutual regard, intellectual and cultural aspirations, moral ideals, fidelity, religious faith, and integrity.

But, even here, we are caught on the horns of a dilemma. For if we are the people who gave the world the exalted idea of marriage as a spiritual union (kiddushin) and of the home as a sanctuary of peace, then we are also the people who today seem to be in the forefront of every contemporary movement whose combined effects shake the Jewish concepts of family to the core. These trends include unrestricted sexual freedom, living together without marriage, and the choice of a growing number of married couples not to have children. They also include a zooming rate of intermarriage and divorce, easy and legal access to birth control devices and abortion as well as profound changes in the role of women in our society.

None of these developments was intended to weaken the

institution of the family. On the contrary, some—like the women's movement and abortion rights—are presented as means to enlarge freedom and thus strengthen family life in the long run. But, in the meantime—in the here and now—the Jewish family is reeling at its very foundations while the American family in general is undergoing a drastic and startling culture shock. Old values are being sharply modified or recast in totally new ways. New values are emerging. Will there be a Jewish family of the future, and what will it be?

What are these new values? They include smaller families; our birth rate is the lowest of any ethnic or religious group in the United States; we are not even reproducing ourselves. Moreover, within the large majority of Jewish homes, American secular values prevail. Television, sports, and the automobile have more influence on Jewish family life than do Hillel, Deborah, Isaiah, and Moses. More heed is paid to the analyst than to the rabbi or even to God. Divorce—once rare and frowned upon—is sharply on the rise and is as common among Jews as among non-Jews. Similarly, drinking, extra-marital sex, and the use of drugs have increased dramatically in the past decade. The traditional family structure has changed. Elderly parents often live in a home for the aged or reside far away from their children.

Much of the self-centeredness of the "Me Decade" is reflected in the mood of the American Jewish family of today, threatening to overpower the strict religious and moral rules of yesterday, commanding fidelity, purity, obedience, truth, and morality. Does all this suggest a temporary fad which will disappear in time? Or is the Jewish family truly becoming an "endangered species" before our unseeing eyes?

WOMEN

The demands of Jewish women for full equality pose a dilemma for traditional Judaism. Despite occasional Jewish heroines such as Deborah in the Bible and the psalmist's praise of the wife and mother as a "woman of valor," it is clear that Jewish tradition followed the cultural pattern of contemporary civilization, which placed women in an inferior position to men. Jewish tradition was considerate toward women; husbands were enjoined to honor their wives and to treat them sensitively. But there is no question that kindness and solicitude did not add up to legal equality.

Jewish law is male-oriented. Within the framework of halachah, Jewish law, women can neither vote nor are they permitted to serve as witnesses. They can not participate as part of the minyan, the traditional group of ten people required for public worship. They can attend services only as spectators, separated from men behind a partition (mechitzah). Traditionally observant Jewish males recite this blessing each morning: "Praised be the Eternal our God, Ruling Spirit of the Universe, who did not make me a woman." A Jewish religious court (bet din) rules on matters of personal status in accordance with this distinct difference in the legal status of men and women. Accordingly, the wife is the "legal property" of her husband who "acquires" her in marriage and who alone has the right to "release" her by divorce.

In Israel today, matters of personal status such as marriage, divorce, child custody, inheritance, and others are subject to halachah (Jewish law) and are administered by the Orthodox rabbinate. It does not matter that a person considers himself or herself "not religious": there is no civil authority to which one can turn.

As equal rights within Judaism are demanded by women in Israel, in America, and wherever Jews live, Orthodoxy will have to resolve the dilemma between traditional law and the rising tide for women's rights. Conservative Judaism, too, has failed as a movement to fully come to terms with the issue of women's religious equality. Women may now be counted as part of a minyan in Conservative synagogues and may also be called to read from the Torah, but the Jewish Theological Seminary (Conservative) still refuses to ordain women rabbis or cantors.

For Reform Jews, this particular dilemma does not exist. Reform does not regard halachah as binding but only as a guide to individual conduct. Reform, from its inception, was based squarely on equality of the sexes. Men and women pray together and are encouraged to participate in all aspects of religious life. But, until recently, full equality did not obtain in practice, and it still does not completely exist even today. Women are now being ordained as rabbis; in a few years, more than half of the rabbinic and cantorial students of Hebrew Union College will be women. Increasingly, women are serving as temple presidents, cantors, educators, on congregational boards, and in the national movement. The Reform movement has a way to go, but it is moving toward full equality. Still, there is a dilemma for liberal Jews!

The picture of legal equality conceals deep-rooted sexism in custom and practice which still prevents the full participation of women in liberal Judaism. Of the 200 members of the Board of Trustees of the Union of American Hebrew Congregations (UAHC) in 1978, only 22 were women. Women have the right to be called to the Torah, but few are called. Bar Mitzvah is still widely regarded as somehow more significant than Bat Mitzvah. Women are often still relegated to the post of recording secretary, to work in the kitchen, or to secondary positions of leadership. Many Jewish textbooks still contain much sexist terminology and women are still largely "written out of history." The UAHC's Department of Publications is a shining exception in this matter. It has definite guidelines against the use of sex-discriminative terms and concepts.

Many congregations are as yet unprepared to have a woman rabbi on their bimah. Jewish professional women frequently are paid considerably less than men doing the same work. Will the congregation which hires a woman as the second rabbi allow her to become the senior person when a vacancy occurs?

What can be done to narrow this gap between our professed aims and our practice? How can we raise the consciousness of women and men to respond to what is perhaps the most profound revolution of our time? For in the end it is not what we

SAY that will count. What will be required is a more equal division of household duties and child rearing in the Jewish home as a first step to bring about the fullest expression of religious, cultural, and intellectual contributions of women to the service of the Jewish and the general community.

ZERO POPULATION GROWTH

Jewish anxiety about women's rights is also tinged with concern about the future of Jewish family life. Our anxiety is intensified by the fear that we may be a vanishing breed. The Jewish birthrate is so low that we are not reproducing ourselves, much less making up for the grave loss of one-third of the entire Jewish people in the Holocaust. When our small birthrate of roughly 2.1 children per family is added to a growing intermarriage rate of about 40 percent, we may be facing a severe crisis. One expert has predicted that, if current statistics are projected to the end of the century, American Jews will have declined from our present population of almost six million to between 25,000 and 900,000. Other experts disagree, contending that a high percentage of the children of intermarried parents are actually raised Jewish; that we may be gaining more than we are losing and that our special Jewish qualities stem from our small numbers in any event.

Of course, numbers are not everything and quantity is not the same as quality. But a shrunken community as predicted by the pessimists would be only .5 percent of the American population instead of the current 2.6 percent and we would undoubtedly lose political and cultural influence. It would also lead to diminished support for Israel and the needs of the national and local community and would probably bring about a serious loss of morale and group spirit.

If the prospect of sharply declining numbers is indeed a serious problem, what steps can be taken now to protect our future?

One answer is that the Jewish community launch a determined educational campaign to persuade young Jews to have larger families. The argument is that we have a moral obligation not to give Hitler a posthumous victory and that this generation must bring the Jewish population back to a level that will guarantee Jewish survival. A Jewish organization has been created called PRU (Jewish Population Regeneration Union) after the biblical expression "p'ru ur'vu," be fruitful and multiply.

Most young Jewish couples reject these suggestions. They contend that the world is suffering from overpopulation which threatens all civilized values and that zero population growth (ZPG) is the moral course for a decent future. Many of them add that the question of how many children to have is a personal and private decision to be made by each couple and not in response to group pressures and ethnic preachment.

In 1978, the Central Conference of American Rabbis (Reform) was faced with the following resolution: "Reform Judaism approves birth control, but we also recognize our obligation to maintain a viable and stable Jewish population. Therefore, couples are encouraged to have at least 2 or 3 children."

The reaction was far from unanimous. Here is an example of what one feminist had to say about the proposal:

"I feel that what the PRU is asking shows a lack of respect for the woman, for the child, and for the family. They are asking Jewish women to become baby machines for the political benefit of the community. Nowhere do they talk about how a woman might feel using her body in this way. Many women and mothers feel burdened and want an opportunity to do more with their lives than simply care for their children and their men. PRU is asking women once again to subordinate their own needs to that of the community and to become either eternal mothers and housewives or baby makers." (Mary Gendler, *Women's American ORT Reporter,* September/October 1976)

If the Jewish community feels it has a right to ask Jewish women to have more children, might it not be heaping guilt on them without achieving any good? And if such a demand is made, are we not obligated to provide a Jewish day-care service to relieve the burden on young mothers who have aspirations to serve themselves and the community in useful careers?

Here is a true dilemma, the conflict of two vital values. Can they be reconciled? If not, to which should be given greater weight?

ABORTION

In the political climate of today, few issues are more potent and devisive than abortion. The mid-term election of '78 saw key congressional and senatorial races turn on this issue. In Iowa, for example, a widely-respected senator, Dick Clark, was defeated after 300,000 "pro-life" leaflets were distributed in churches on the Sunday before election day. In Minnesota, a distinguished legislator, Don Fraser, was defeated in a primary contest in which his support for abortion rights made him a prime target for intense anti-abortion groups. Dozens of other races were deeply influenced by bitter clashes about abortion. Similarly, in New York State, the "Right to Life Party" won more than 100,000 votes for its anti-abortion candidate for governor, assuring this single issue party a place on New York State ballots for the next four years.

The controversy about abortion was preceded by a series of angry confrontations in Congress over repeated efforts to tie anti-abortion legislation to a variety of bills, aimed especially against Medicaid payments for abortion, to make it impossible for poor women to receive abortions at public expense.

Jews overwhelmingly favor the right of free choice in the matter of abortion. But there are differences among Jewish groups as there are among Protestants and Catholics. Orthodox Judaism sides with the Roman Catholic Church in condemning abortion. The Catholic Church leads the campaign against abortion as "murder to the unborn"; Orthodox Jews are its frequent allies in communities throughout America. Reform and Conservative Judaism have taken a clear stand in favor of free choice for women, and rabbinic and lay leaders of these branches play prominent roles in such groups as the Religious Coalition for Abortion Rights.

In testimony before the House of Representatives in 1980, the Reform movement declared its position on abortion clearly and unequivocally:

"The Supreme Court holds that the question of when life begins is a matter of religious belief and not medical or legal fact. We recognize the right of religious groups whose beliefs differ from ours to follow the dictates of their faith. We vigorously oppose the attempts to legislate the particular beliefs of those groups into the law which governs us all. This is a clear violation of the First Amendment. . . .

"We oppose bills aimed at halting medicaid, legal counselling, and family services in abortion-related activities. These restrictions severely discriminate against and penalize the poor who rely on governmental assistance to obtain medical care to which they are legally entitled, including abortion.

"We are opposed to attempts to restrict the right to abortion through constitutional amendments. To establish in the Constitution the view of certain religious groups on the beginning of life has legal implications far beyond the question of abortion. Such amendments would undermine constitutional liberties which protect all Americans."

But Jewish dilemmas remain. Jewish tradition generally holds that a foetus may be destroyed to save the mother's life. But is it not stretching the tradition to assert that it would support abortion on demand? Can Jewish tradition really sanction abortion on economic, psychological, or social grounds? Arguing for the right of free choice in the matter of abortion does not necessarily mean that the grave decision to abort a foetus is either ethical or wise. Abortion may be, and should be, a free choice, but it must be seen as one of the most serious moral decisions a person can ever face.

Abortion presents grave dilemmas both for opponents and proponents. Opponents, claiming fidelity to the right to life for the unborn, often show little concern for life on such matters as capital punishment, gun control, the arms race, and related issues. They frequently help to elect politicians who vote "right" on abortion and wrong on everything else, while their more liberal opponents are defeated by one-issue campaigns.

Those who wage war against abortion also tend to fight measures to alleviate the abortion crisis—sex education, free birth control clinics, and the support services required by poor pregnant women.

Proponents, for their part, tend to make a virtue of abortion. It is one thing to defend the right of free choice; it is another to make a moral good of abortion. Most Americans insist on the right of free choice in smoking; but that doesn't make smoking a good thing. A woman's decision to have an abortion is a profound and grave personal decision. Yet many advocates seem keenly aware of the sanctity of life for whales, deer, and redwood trees, but are somehow casually confident that the first manifestations of human life can be destroyed at will. Anti-abortion Americans may be mistaken and their political impact may be hurtful, but they may also be doing a service by giving the rest of us pause to reconsider the moral and human implications of a dilemma that will not go away.

INTERMARRIAGE—THE BIG DILEMMA

American Jews are as concerned about intermarriage as about any other crisis in their lives. And why not? It could spell the end of the Jewish people. By all accounts, intermarriage rates are high and seem to be still rising, reaching close to 40 percent at the end of the 1970s.

What can be done about it? A central debate in the Jewish community has to do with whether or not a rabbi should officiate at an intermarriage of a Jew and a non-Jew. Orthodox and Conservative rabbis are unanimously opposed, feeling that to put the stamp of Jewish authenticity on such a marriage is to preside over the liquidation of the Jewish people. They regard such a marriage as, not only regrettable, but a "chilul Hashem," a desecration of the God of Israel. Reform rabbis are split on the subject, the majority siding with their traditional colleagues. A minority disagrees, contending that the marriage will take place anyway; that it is better not to drive the couple away completely and that free choice must also be respected.

This is a difficult issue for liberal rabbis, but it is not the only painful dilemma. What happens after that couple is married? Do the rabbi and the rest of the liberal Jewish community reach out to that couple or write them off as lost?

Hundreds of thousands of such intermarried couples exist, and their numbers will rise in the future. The most recent research challenges the assumption that most are lost to Judaism. Indeed, when the wife is Jewish, more than 90 percent of the children of such marriages are raised as Jews; often, the husband drifts into a kind of Jewish lifestyle including some Jewish home observances and Jewish education for the children, and even for the parents. Where the husband is Jewish, 46 percent of the non-Jewish wives "identify" themselves as Jewish. Some 98 percent of intermarried couples where the wife is Jewish and 63 percent where the husband is Jewish intend to provide a "Jewish" religious upbringing for their children.

Tolerance among Americans for interracial and interfaith marriages has substantially increased over the last decade, according to a Gallup poll in the late 1970s. The poll indicated that 36 percent approved of interracial marriages in contrast to 20 percent, who had approved in 1968. Similarly, in 1968, 59 percent had approved of intermarriage between a Jew and a non-Jew, and that approval had risen to 69 percent.

Intermarriage is a serious problem, but there are also opportunities for Jews to reach out to men and women never before approached. Some innovative proposals were made by Rabbi Alexander Schindler, president of the Union of American Hebrew Congregations, at a meeting of the UAHC Board of Trustees in 1978. You will find them and the article "And the Stranger Who Dwells Among You . . ." by Lydia Kukoff (reprinted in the chapter, "Interfaith Relations") interesting to read and discuss.

PRESIDENTIAL ADDRESS

By Rabbi Alexander M. Schindler, Union of American Hebrew Congregations, Board of Trustees, December 2, 1978, Houston, Texas.

It is good to be here, my friends, good to be reunited with the leaders of Reform Jewry, with men and women from many congregations and communities but of one faith, bound together by a common sacred cause. It is not my intention this night to give you a comprehensive report of the Union's activities—but rather to offer a resolution which recommends the creation of an agency within our movement which will earnestly and urgently confront some of the problems of intermarriage in an effort to turn the tide, which threatens to sweep us away, into directions which might enable us to recover our numbers and to recharge our inner strength.

I begin with recognition of a reality: the tide of intermarriage is running against us. As a rabbi committed to the survival of the Jewish people, it pains me to say so, but this is the reality and we must face it. But facing reality does not mean its complacent acceptance. It does not mean that we must prepare to sit *shivah* for the American Jewish community. Quite the contrary! Facing reality means coming to grips with it, determining to reshape it.

Jewish education is usually held forth as the healing balm, and to a certain extent this is true. The statistics which brought us the bad news also gave us proof of that: The incidence of intermarriage is in inverse proportion to the intensity of Jewish rearing. The more Jewish education the less the likelihood of intermarriage. But it isn't always so.

The Union is justly proud of its program of formal and informal education. The bulk of our resources and energies are expended in this realm: We run camps and Israel tours and youth retreats. We conduct college weekends and kallahs and teacher training institutes. We create curricula and texts and educational aids.

No less than 45,000 youngsters participate in Union-led programs each and every year, their Jewish literacy enhanced, their Jewish commitments deepened. Among them are your rabbis and leaders of tomorrow; among them, the guides and scholars of our future.

Among them are also many who will intermarry—hundreds, if not thousands, of them. We live in an open society. Intermarriage is the sting which comes to us with the honey of our freedom.

Yet, even when our children intermarry, Jewish education remains a crucial factor. Because all the studies agree that in most such marriages it is the JEWISH partner who ultimately determines whether or not there will be a conversion to Judaism and whether the children will or will not be reared as Jews. It is the Jewish partner whose will prevails . . . provided, of course, he or she chooses to exercise that will.

To put the matter differently: the fact of intermarriage does not in and of itself lead to a decline in the Jewish population. That decline depends on what the Jews who are involved in the intermarriage actually do.

Jewish education is important then but, important as it is, tonight I do not make a plea for its extension and intensification, although I might well make it, to stem the tide of intermarriage. But rather it is the plea that we as a movement can and should be doing far more than we are doing now to turn the tide around in our favor.

The conversion of the non-Jewish partner-to-be is clearly the first choice and we make a reasonable effort to attain it. The Union offers "Introduction to Judaism" courses in most major communities and congregational rabbis spend countless hours giving instruction. Jewish ideas are explored, ceremonies described, history and Hebrew are taught. But there, by and large, our efforts come to an end. Immediately after the marriage ceremony between the born Jew and the newly converted Jewish partner, we drop the couple and leave them to fend for themselves. We do not help them to make a Jewish home, to rear their children Jewishly, to grapple with their peculiar problems. More serious still, we do not really embrace them, enable them to feel a close kinship with our people.

If the truth be told, we often alienate them in a kind of reverse discrimination, we question their motivations (as if to say that only a madman would choose to be a Jew and so there must be an ulterior motive); or we regard them as being somehow less Jewish (what irony in this for they know more about Judaism than most born Jews); and to the end of their days we refer to them as "converts," if not worse.

Don't for a moment think these whispers behind the back aren't heard and do not hurt. Listen to these lines written to a colleague recently:

Dear Steve:

I know that I personally resent being referred to as a convert—a word that by now is alien to my heart. My conversion *process* was nearly ten years ago—I have been a *Jew* for a long time now. I am distinctly aware of my original background and birthright. This does not alter my identity as a Jew. If one is curious about from where I come or if indeed "am I really Jewish," the answer is categorically "Yes, I'm really Jewish—a Jew by choice."

I shall continue to grow and to search as a Jew. My "conversion process" was just that—a process which ended with the ceremony. From then on I was a Jew.

Yours,
Jane

Jews-by-choice have special needs and we need special guidance on how to meet them. There is the problem of how to *deal* with the *Jewish*-born partner who is *indifferent* to his or her faith.

Then there is the matter of the *past*; the new Jews may have broken with it, but in human terms they cannot forget their non-Jewish parents or families and at certain times of the year, on Christmas and Easter, they are bound to feel ambivalences. Finally, those who choose to become Jews quickly learn that they have adopted something far more than a religion; they have adopted a people with its own history, its way of life.

We certainly need them to be a part of this people, for they can add no strength to us if they are only individuals who share our beliefs rather than members of our *community* of faith. Newcomers to Judaism must embark, in effect, on a long-term naturalization process and they require knowledgeable and sympathetic guides to help them along the way.

Let the newly-formed Commission show us how we can provide this special and sensitive assistance, how these couples can be made to feel that the Jewish community welcomes them and *that they are fully equal members of the synagogue family.*

This point merits the emphasis of repetition. Jews by choice are Jews in the full meaning of the term. The great Sage Moses Maimonides wrote in answer to a convert's query:

"You ask whether you, being a convert, may speak the prayers: 'God and God of our Fathers' and 'Guardian of Israel who has brought us out of the land of Egypt.'

"Pronounce all prayers as they are written and do not change a word. Your prayers and your blessings should be the same as any other Jew. . . .

"This above all: do not think of your origin. *We* may be descended from Abraham, Isaac, and Jacob, but *your* descent is from the Almighty himself. . . ."

Now, not all non-Jewish partners of an intermarriage convert to Judaism as we so well know. The majority, in fact, do not. Statistics are hard to come by, but what we have suggests these facts: A preponderance of intermarriage involves Jewish husbands and non-Jewish wives and upward to 40 percent of these women formally accept our faith. In that smaller grouping involving non-Jewish husbands and Jewish wives, the rate of conversion is not much more than 3 percent. However, something extremely interesting has come to light. Social scientists have uncovered a "Jewish drift," the phenomenon of a "turning" to our faith. Their research has established that *nearly 50 percent of non-Jewish husbands, though not formal-*

ly embracing Judaism, by their own description, nonetheless regard themselves as Jews.

This brings me to my second proposal: I believe that our Reform congregations must do everything possible to draw into Jewish life the non-Jewish spouse of a mixed marriage. If non-Jewish partners can be brought *more actively* into Jewish communal life, perhaps they themselves will initiate the process of conversion or at the very least we will assure that their children will be reared as Jews.

We can begin by removing those "not wanted" signs from our hearts. We reject intermarriage—not the intermarried. If Jews-by-choice often feel alienated by our attitudes we can imagine how we make the non-Jewish spouses of our children feel.

We can also remove the barriers to a fuller participation in many of our congregations. Even halachah offers more than ample leeway to allow the non-Jewish partner to join in most of our ceremonial and life-cycle events. Halachah permits a non-Jew to be in the temple, to sing in the choir, to recite the blessing over the Sabbath and festival candles, and even to handle the Torah. There is no law which forbids a non-Jew to be buried in a Jewish cemetery.

As for the children born of such a marriage, if the mother is Jewish the child is regarded as fully Jewish. But if she is not, then even Orthodoxy, if the non-Jewish mother agrees, permits the circumcision of the boy, his enrollment in religious school, and his right to the Torah on the occasion of his Bar Mitzvah and to be considered a full Jew thereafter. All this is possible under Orthodoxy. How much the more so under Reform! If we put our best minds to it, we will find many other ways which can bolster our efforts in this direction.

Why should a movement which from its very birthhour insisted on the full equality of men and women in religious life accept the principle that Jewish lineage is valid through the maternal line alone? There may even be substantial support in our tradition for the validity of Jewish lineage also through the paternal line.

By way of illustration: a leading member of the United States Senate is not a Jew, although he was born a Jew. His father was Jewish. His mother converted from one of the Christian denominations. He was circumcised, reared as a Jew, and attended religious school. When the time of his Bar Mitzvah approached, the rabbi refused to recognize the validity of his mother's conversion and did not allow the boy to recite the blessings over the Torah. Embarrassed and enraged, the entire family converted to Christianity. This is why a leading United States lawmaker is not a Jew today.

I am not proposing a resolution of this paternal-maternal line issue at this time. But, there is a possibility to bring our tradition in line with modern need. A special Task Force, for whose creation I call, should pursue this delicate matter.

I have a third proposal to make on the subject of our declining Jewish population in America: I believe that it is time for our movement to launch a carefully conceived Outreach Program aimed at all Americans who are unchurched and who are seeking roots in religion.

Let me not hide my true intent through the use of cosmetic language. Unabashedly and urgently, I call on our members to resume their time-honored vocation and to become champions for Judaism. Champions for Judaism—these words imply not just passive acceptance but affirmative action.

I do not envisage that we conduct our Outreach Program as a kind of travelling religious circus. I see a dignified and responsible approach: The establishment of information centers in many places, well-publicized courses in our synagogues, and the development of suitable publications to serve these purposes. In other words, I suggest that we respond openly and positively to those God-seekers who voluntarily ask for our knowledge.

Nor do I suggest that we strive to turn people away from religions of their choice with the boast that ours is the only true and valid faith. I want to reach a different audience entirely, the unchurched, those reared in non-religious homes or those who have become disillusioned with their taught beliefs, the seekers after truth who require a religion which encourages all questions, and especially the alienated and the rootless who need the warmth and comfort of a people well-known for its close family ties.

The notion that Judaism is not a propagating faith is wide of the truth. That may have been true for the last four centuries, but it is not true for the four thousand years before that.

Abraham was a convert and our tradition lauds his missionary zeal. Isaiah enjoined us to be a "light unto the nations" and insisted that God's house be a "house of prayer for *all* peoples." Ruth of Moab, a heathen by birth, became the ancestor of King David.

During the Maccabean period, Jewish proselytizing activity reached its zenith . . . schools for missionaries were established and by the beginning of the Christian era they had succeeded in converting 10 percent of the population of the Roman Empire—or roughly four million people.

True, the Talmud insists that we test the sincerity of the convert's motivations, by discouraging them, by warning them of the hardships which they will have to endure as Jews. But the Talmud then adds that while we are "to push converts away with the left hand" we ought to "draw them *near* with the right."

After Christianity became the state religion of the Roman Empire and, later, again, when Islam conquered the world, Jews were forbidden to seek converts or to accept them. The death penalty was set for Gentiles who became Jews and for the Jew who welcomed them. Many were actually burned at the stake. This served to cool our conversionist ardor somewhat. Still it was not until the sixteenth century that we abandoned all proselytizing efforts and our rabbis began their systematic rejection of those who sought to join us.

But we live in America today. No repressive laws restrain us. The fear of persecution no longer inhibits us. There is no earthly reason now why we cannot reassume our ancient vocation and open our arms wide to all newcomers.

Why are we so hesitant? Are we ashamed? Must one really be a madman to choose Judaism? Let us recapture our self-esteem! Let us demonstrate our confidence in those values which our faith enshrines!

Millions of Americans are searching for something. Tragically, many of these seekers have fallen prey to mystical cults which literally enslave them.

Judaism offers life, not death. It teaches free will, not surrender of body and soul to another human being. The Jew prays directly to God, not through intermediaries who stand between them and God. Judaism is a religion of hope and not despair, it insists that people and society are perfectible. Judaism has an enormous amount of wisdom and experience to offer this troubled world, and we Jews ought to be proud to speak about it, frankly, freely, and with dignity.

There is something different in the world today and we all can feel it. The very air we breathe is tense, a wind blows through space, and the treetops are astir. Men and women are restless, but not with the restlessness of those who have lost their way in the world and have surrendered to despair. But rather with the hopeful questing of those who want to find a way and are determined to reach it. It is a search for true values and deeper, more personal, meaning. It is a purposeful adventure of the spirit.

The prophet Amos spoke of this search when he said:

"Behold the day will come, says the Lord, that I will send a famine in the land not a famine of bread nor a thirst for water but of hearing the words of the Lord."

My friends, we Jews possess the water which can slake the thirst, the bread which can sate this great hunger. Let us offer it freely, proudly—for *our* well-being and for the sake of those who earnestly seek what is ours to give.

HOMOSEXUALITY

In 1977, the issue of homosexual rights burst on the nation's consciousness as a major issue of minority rights and social justice. In Dade County, Florida (the Miami area), the City

Council had earlier adopted a unanimous resolution, making it illegal to deny civil rights to any person on account of his or her sexual preference. Similar civil rights measures had earlier been adopted without too much fuss in other cities.

It was, therefore, surprising when a massive, expensive, and emotional campaign was launched to reverse the measure through a public referendum. Led by the singer, Anita Bryant, the campaign appealed to public fears that homosexual teachers would molest small children in the public schools, that homosexual marriages would receive societal sanction, and that the integrity of the family and the sanctity of marriage would be undermined. Proponents of the rights measure insisted that the gay minority, as others, required protection against harassment and discrimination; that intolerance and bigotry against homosexuals leads to denial of their civil rights; that passage of similar rights measures in other communities had resulted in none of the dire consequences predicted by the opponents.

Fundamentalist religious groups were joined by right-wing political forces who linked homosexual rights with pornography, the passage of the Equal Rights Amendment, and abortion reform as part of a "liberal" conspiracy to destroy American institutions. They called on Christians to take a stand against "paganism." They invoked the biblical injunction against homosexuality as an "abomination." Anita Bryant proclaimed: "If God would have wanted us to approve homosexuality, He would have created Adam and Bruce!"

The supporters of rights of homosexuals invoked the memory of Nazi persecution. Using dreadful photographs of Nazi brutality, they pointedly asserted that Hitler assaulted homosexuals and gypsies before moving on to Jews and other minorities. This was an obvious appeal to the large Jewish community and to Jewish emotions.

The final vote was a resounding defeat of the gay rights measure. Every ethnic, racial, and religious group—except one—voted heavily to kill the measure. Only the Jews cast a majority of their votes for the rights bill. But even the Jewish community was deeply and bitterly divided. Reform rabbis strongly supported the measure, citing the official stand of the Commission on Social Action:

"We believe that all people are children of God, regardless of their sexual orientation, and that homosexual persons have a full and equal claim with all other persons upon the love, acceptance, and pastoral concern of rabbis and synagogues.

"We express our conviction that homosexual persons are entitled to equal protection of the law with all other citizens in areas which include employment and housing, and we call upon our society to see that such protection is provided.

"We also believe that private sexual acts between consenting adults are not the proper province of government and enforcement agencies."

Most Orthodox spokesmen, feeling bound by the clear stand of the Bible, joined the opposition. So did the most influential Conservative rabbi in Miami Beach. After the referendum, these rabbis must have felt more than a little uneasy when Miss Bryant hailed the "Christian crusaders" who had beaten back the forces of evil.

There was much heat and emotional overkill on both sides, but the issues raised in Miami are of national importance and require cool analysis by persons concerned with social justice. On the simple issue of equal rights, no person of good will can gainsay the elemental justice of the gay case. Is a person to be treated as an outcast because he or she has a deviant sexual preference? On the other hand, some homosexuals seemed to be demanding something more than mere civil rights—an affirmation by society that homosexuality be viewed as an approved alternative life style. Many persons are not prepared to make such an endorsement. Some experts continue to regard homosexuality as an illness, even though the American Psychiatric Association has voted that it no longer regards it as such. Others, willing to protect homosexual rights, believe that placing it on the same moral plane as heterosexuality will jeopardize the basis of marriage and family and in the long run threaten the survival of the human species.

The anti-homosexual forces, mobilized first in Miami, are now mounting a powerful offensive to sweep gay rights legislation off the boards throughout the nation. In cities as dissimilar as St. Paul, Wichita, and Spokane, these forces have overwhelmed gays and their supporters. In California, a referendum sought to deny gays the right to become teachers in public schools. It was defeated.

For us, as Jews, the issue is even more complicated because the halachic prohibition cannot be dismissed merely as primitive and inhumane. Liberal Jews must, at least, consider and reinterpret it in the light of present knowledge and moral standards. It is not easy. Our communities and courts are facing the question of the right of gay public school teachers. What about rabbis? Should our seminaries be prepared to admit avowed homosexuals? If not, would that be a denial of civil rights? If yes, would that be a denial of basic Jewish teachings?

The Reform community has begun to face the question of homosexual Jews, recognizing that a not insignificant proportion of the homosexual population (estimated by Kinsey to be 10 percent of the total population) is comprised of Jewish men and women. Are these people to be excluded from the Jewish fold? Is homosexuality to be regarded by us as an emotional disorder, a sin, or an alternative lifestyle? Can we be humane toward homosexuals while refusing to condone homosexuality? Should sexual orientation be a matter of indifference to society? Can the Jewish community, with its emphasis on family and historic continuity, ignore the implications for future generations of sanctioning homosexuality? If we condone a gay congregation, will we be asked to condone homosexual marriages within Jewish life?

The latter issue was forced on the UAHC when a newly-formed congregation in Los Angeles, made up primarily of homosexuals, applied for membership. This is a serious congregation of Jews committed to study, prayer, worship, and the Jewish people. The individuals who comprised it had found themselves uncomfortable in straight congregations with their natural emphasis on heterosexual couples and families. They wanted their own congregation, and they wanted to be admitted as members of the Reform community. The UAHC carefully explored all aspects of the problem, including the diverse opinions of Reform scholars, who probed the halachic tradition and its relevance.

Here are three divergent "responsa" (opinions based on Jewish law), from three respected rabbis, which the Union examined in the process of making its decision.

TRADITION FORBIDS TO EXCLUDE THEM

There is no question that the Bible considers homosexuality to be a grave sin. The rabbi who organized this congregation said, in justifying himself, that, being Reform, we are not bound by the halachah of the Bible. It well may be that we do not consider ourselves bound by all the ritual and ceremonial laws of Scriptures but we certainly revere the ethical attitudes and judgments of the Bible. In Leviticus 18:22, homosexuality is considered to be "an abomination." So, too, in Leviticus 20:13. If the Bible calls it an abomination, it means that it is more than violation of a law; it reveals a deep-rooted ethical attitude. How deep-rooted this aversion is can be seen from the fact that, although Judaism developed in the Near East, which is notorious for the prevalence of homosexuality, Jews kept away from such acts. Opposition to homosexuality was more than a biblical law; it was a deep-rooted way of life of the Jewish people. Therefore homosexual acts cannot be brushed aside, by saying that we do not follow biblical laws. Homosexuality runs counter to the principles of Jewish life; from the point of view of Judaism, people who practice homosexuality are to be deemed sinners.

Does it mean, therefore, that we should exclude them from the congregation and compel them to form their own religious fellowship in congregations of their own? No! The very contrary is true. It is forbidden to exclude them into a separate congregation. As Jews, we must pray side by side with the sinners. In other words, not only do we *not* exclude sinners, we are actually forbidden to do so; they are a necessary part of the congregation.

This throws light on the present situation. We do not exclude them. We are forbidden by our tradition to do so. They are excluding themselves; and it is our duty to ask, why are they doing it? Why do they want to commit the further sin of "separating themselves from the congregation"?

Part of their wish is, of course, due to the "Gay Liberation" movement. Homosexuals, fighting the laws which they deem unjust, take a strong stand in behalf of their status to gain formal recognition from all possible groups. If they can get the Union of American Hebrew Congregations to acknowledge their right to form separate congregations, it will bolster their claim for other rights.

It seems to me, also, that it is not unfair to add another motive for their desire to be in one congregation: in this way they know each other and are available to each other, just as they now meet in separate bars in the large cities. What, then, of young boys who perhaps have only a partial homosexual tendency, who will now be available to these homosexuals? Are we not thereby committing the sin of "aiding and abetting sinners"?

To sum up: Homosexuality is deemed in Jewish tradition to be a sin, not only in law but in Jewish life practice. Nevertheless, it would be in direct contravention to Jewish law to keep sinners out of the congregation. To isolate them into a separate congregation and thus increase their mutual availability is certainly wrong.

Rabbi Solomon B. Freehof

RABBIS MUST DEFINE THEIR OBLIGATIONS

I do not believe that we should encourage the formation of homosexual congregations. Wherever possible, we should urge homosexual Jews to integrate into existing congregations. But that means that we must be more responsive to their presence among us and to create a climate of greater acceptability for them.

But under present conditions this is not a realistic possibility for the near future. Therefore, homosexuals who want their own congregations should be assisted by the Union. For on the simplest level such synagogues provide an opportunity for homosexuals to worship in a setting more comfortable to them and to us: until existing congregations are able to accept them in their homosexuality, having their own congregations will serve a vital function in helping them to achieve status and dignity as Jews and as homosexuals.

It is easy for me to talk about the obligations of the Union of American Hebrew Congregations, but I hesitate to tell other rabbis what their obligations are. I believe that each rabbi must define the nature and content of his or her own rabbinic obligations. We should strive to make it possible for a rabbi to serve such a congregation without fear of reproach or reprisal. The entire Reform movement has an obligation to work in this direction and, if such congregations seek admission and meet the criteria for Union membership, they should, of course, be accepted.

Rabbi Leonard Beerman
Leo Baeck Temple, Los Angeles

NO SEPARATE CONGREGATIONS

Jewish law regards homosexuality as a capital offense to be punished by stoning (Lev. 20:13). Biblical and rabbinic law concerning the homosexual is based on several assumptions: the homosexual acts out of free will; he/she is a willful rebel who flaunts the natural law and the law of God. We, however, know today that in the overwhelming number of cases homosexuals are not willful rebels. They are that way from birth or became homosexuals in early childhood or adolescence. We should, therefore, in the light of our present knowledge, treat homosexuals as people who act under duress and merit all the sympathy, consideration, and kindness that the halachah extends to a victim who is forced to act under duress.

Our attitude toward the homosexual would, therefore, have to be as follows:

They are to be treated as victims and are to be accepted without moral judgment in terms of personal guilt or sin, and every form of sympathetic understanding should be extended to them.

Homosexuality cannot be considered normal. One who chooses homosexuality is, from a Jewish point of view, committing a sin.

Since children can be seduced into homosexuality and adolescents can be influenced toward conduct which will remain with them all of their lives, it is the right of society to protect minors from homosexual seduction through legislation. It is also the moral obligation of parents to protect children from such influence.

If we are not to judge homosexuals as willful sinners, we must extend to them the privilege of joining a congregation. Jewish religion demands that we welcome them and treat them with the kindness and consideration extended to anyone who desires to join a synagogue.

Any group of Jews has the right to organize and to form a congregation. The goals of the group must, however, be in consonance with the purposes of a synagogue as defined by the historic Jewish experience—the ideals and moral values of Judaism.

It is clear that a congregation which uses the criterion of homosexuality as the basis for membership and as the basis for its organization is contrary to the fundamental religious spirit of Judaism.

The answer to your question, then, "Should we encourage the formation of separate congregations for homosexuals" is definitely in the negative. The synagogue should help in integrating homosexuals in the religious life of the community, not be a vehicle for isolating them, and, if a "homosexual congregation seeks membership in the Union," it should not be accepted. . . .

Dr. Eugene Mihaly
Hebrew Union College-Jewish Institute of Religion

In 1974, the UAHC Board voted, after exhaustive debate, to admit the congregation to membership, provided it was open to all Jews and not only gay Jews. This decision was denounced by some and warmly supported by others. It also gave encouragement to many gay Jews who seek the support of their fellow Jews and who contend that the principle of "Kelal Yisrael" must be a tent of Jacob ample enough to embrace all Jews regardless of race, philosophy, or sexual preference.

5

INTERFAITH RELATIONS

If Jews did not actually invent interfaith relations in America, we certainly played a principal role in creating them. Reform Judaism, especially, regarded the cultivation of friendly ties with Christian groups as a vital aspect of the Jewish mission in an America based upon mutual respect and religious pluralism. Rabbis established cooperative relationships with the more liberal local Protestant ministers; until recent years, the Roman Catholic Church remained aloof from interreligious affairs. The (Reform) Jewish Chautauqua Society sent rabbis and Jewish scholars to college campuses to share information about Jews and Judaism with Christian students.

In recent decades, interfaith relations have undergone sweeping changes, especially within the Roman Catholic Church which has gone so far as to reinterpret some of its fundamental teachings to eliminate the anti-Semitic bias derived from historic interpretations of the Christian Scripture. Moreover, after Vatican Council II, convened by Pope John XXIII in 1963, the Church—which had spurned interfaith contact for centuries—began to establish friendly relations with Protestants as well as with Jews. Priests exchanged pulpits with rabbis. Roman Catholics frequently took the lead in summoning Protestants and Catholics to interreligious social action for common causes in the community. Textbooks in Catholic religious schools were examined to eliminate—or at least soften—passages offensive to Jewish sensibilities. The Roman Catholic Church in the US maintains an office for the improvement of Catholic-Jewish relations, which seeks to stimulate dialogue, exchanges, joint action, and mutual respect.

How can such positive developments represent a dilemma for Jews who helped to create the National Conference of Christians and Jews and whose history in America has been one of warm advocacy of closer contact among religious groups?

DO THE TIES STILL BIND US?

The answer is strange and ironic. At the very moment when the Catholic Church came out in eager pursuit of its "brothers and sisters of other faiths," American Jews—once the most universal, the most open, and the most avid for interfaith efforts—were heading in the opposite direction. While Catholics were streaming out of their parochial concerns and rushing toward involvement in civil rights and the peace movement, Jews were busy retreating from the universal agenda to their own particular Jewish issues of Israel and Soviet Jewry. In a historic switch, two major faith groups virtually exchanged roles, passing like two ships in the night.

The Roman Catholic revolution has many origins, including the startling leadership of Pope John XXIII who opened the windows of the Church to let fresh air and new ideas blow in to a Church which had grown musty and out of touch with changing times. But what had happened to the Jews? What had happened to weaken the legendary Jewish passion to nurture the good will of the Christians? In a word: *disappointment.* The Jewish heart was broken, not only by the awesome fact of the Holocaust, but by the devastating realization that, with some exceptions, Christians had been silent accomplices to the slaughter of the innocents. Many Jews who survived the Holocaust never recovered from that spiritual wound of shattered faith.

Others, buoyed by the creation of Israel and the flourishing of the American Jewish community in the aftermath of World War II, devoted themselves to cementing Christian-Jewish relationships, especially in the suburbs where both Judaism and Christianity boomed in the postwar decades. Many new Jewish congregations were born in the suburban church which hospitably extended its facilities to the fledgling synagogue until it could find the resources to erect its own building. The minister and the rabbi often became good friends, allies in battles for civil rights and church-state separation, and often their congregations held joint services, study courses, dialogues, and social action projects together.

Then came the Six Day War in Israel. Jews, everywhere, felt a sudden chill. Was the Jewish people again to face genocide, this time at the hands of Arabs pledged to Jewish extermination? And where were the voices of humanity? Where were the voices of Christianity this time around? With a few exceptions, ominous silence reigned once again. Jews, feeling in their bones their own vulnerability as Israel was surrounded by hostile and threatening forces, suddenly felt that sinking sense of being in galut (exile) once again. And they felt a disappointment, edged with anger, at what they saw to be vast indifference by their neighbors to the ultimate peril to the Jewish people, only one generation after the Holocaust. Even when the Israelis achieved their spectacular and triumphant victory, the widespread feeling of having been let down by the civilized world—and especially the Christian world—lingered in the Jewish consciousness. Inevitably, Jews lost their appetite for interfaith activities, drifting away from some programs, maintaining some others without enthusiasm; their hearts no longer in such efforts, they turned their energies to the immediate tasks of the Jewish agenda.

Was the indictment of the Christian world fair? Yes and no. It is true that most Christian bodies did not speak up for Israel when Egypt's Nasser was publicly preparing a noose for the destruction of the Jewish state and when the trembling Jewish sense of solitude deepened. But some individual Christian leaders rallied to the Jewish cause—and continue to do so. Moreover, public opinion polls showed that the American people were overwhelmingly pro-Israel, and obviously American Christians made up the bulk of that support. And, it must also be said that it is unrealistic of Jews to expect non-Jews to be as aware and responsive to Jewish hurts as we are ourselves. Did we Jews always speak up on the great moral issues of the civil war in Northern Ireland, the conflict in Rhodesia, or turmoil in Chile? We Jews have a right to our sensitivity. But it can verge on paranoia to denounce Christians for being self-interested and slow to respond to Jewish issues when, in truth, we Jews also often stand idly by other people's calamities, sometimes right in our home communities.

We demand that Christian bodies cleanse their liturgies and textbooks of anti-Jewish stereotypes. It is proper for us to make such demands because we know that centuries of Christian teachings, denigrating Jews and chronicling the so-called Jewish crime of "deicide" (killing God), prepared the ground for Hitler's madness. But are we Jews falling into our own set of prejudices? Are we nurturing anti-Christian stereotypes? Are we as scrupulous that Jewish textbooks treat non-Jews as we expect to be treated? In our private lives, do we reflect respect for other faiths in everyday personal attitudes and conduct? We have a deep antagonism to intermarriage, and our concern is fully justified by our will to survive as a Jewish people. But we do not have to derogate Christians in the process.

There are many persons who believe that the Jewish drift away from interfaith relations is a serious mistake. If Christians do not really understand our passionate involvement with Israel, if they can not understand the *religious* basis for our love of Israel, we cannot hope to make them more sensitive except by face-to-face dialogue, discussion, and education. Not only that. American Jewry needs the understanding and support of

American Christians on the issues most urgent to us—US support for Israel and for Soviet Jewry. It is against our best interest to turn our backs on allies and to nurse our own hurts in isolation. We *need* to be involved for our *own* sakes. Moreover, we Jews have an equally real stake in what happens to *America!* Despite our profound solidarity with Israel, our future will be shaped, in large measure, by what America becomes. If America becomes an apartheid society boiling with racial strife, or a regressive police state, we Jews will have no future here. It is in our own interest to work with all possible allies, Jews and non-Jews alike, to solve social problems and to build a decent community in an open and compassionate America. It is not only in our own interest; it is also the foundation of our Jewish religious and ethical heritage. We are also Jews for the sake of humanity!

MISSIONIZING

Another major irritant in interfaith relations is the Christian addiction to seek converts to Christianity among Jews. Here, too, Jewish sensitivity is not surprising. Throughout the centuries of Christian dominance of the Western world, Jews were subjected to every conceivable form of persecution and harassment and, at its worst, the Church's Inquisition imposed forced conversions on millions of Jews at pain of death.

In modern times, major Christian groups have reevaluated their positions on missionizing Jews. Major Protestant denominations have declared that, while they have a Christian obligation to be witness to Christ and to bring the "good news" of salvation to all people, they will no longer single out Jews as the special target of missionary activities. The Roman Catholic Church has gone full circle, asserting that it is no longer Church policy to seek to convert Jews, acknowledging for the first time that God's Covenant with the Jews has not been revoked, even though Jews have not accepted the divinity of the "Christ."

THE THREAT OF THE CULTS

But, ironically, while the mainline churches have abandoned —or at least tempered—their missionary campaigns toward Jews, fundamentalist Christian groups, together with emergent exotic cults, have mounted feverish missionary efforts to win Jewish souls in America. These efforts have infuriated and alarmed Jews and further intensified Jewish resistance to Christian-Jewish relations.

Among the cults are the Unification Church ("Moonies"), the Children of God, the Church of Scientology, the Forever Family, the Hare Krishna, the Divine Light Mission, Jews for Jesus, and others. What is a cult? Definitions are elusive and subjective, but it would be safe to say that a cult is a group that reflects the following characteristics: It is a group of people who obey a living leader, usually a dominant male figure, who makes absolute claims to being divine, the messiah, God's agent on earth, omniscient and infallible. It is a group in which membership depends on literal acceptance of the leader's claims to divinity and unquestioned obedience to his doctrines. It is a group that is undemocratic and peculiar in its religious practice. Some of the cults are anti-Semitic.

Jewish young people are heavily represented in these cults. Nobody has precise figures, but students of cults generally agree that Jews seem over-represented in them. Why are Jewish youngsters so susceptible to such bizarre groups? What does this say about American Jewish life, about the Jewish family, education, the synagogue?

Young people join cults for a variety of reasons that may have nothing to do with the dogmas of the group. Loneliness, a hunger for friendship, disillusionment with reason and science, a need for moral authority, a yearning for a sense of purpose —all these enter into a person's readiness to join. Cult recruiting consists of "love-bombing" of vulnerable, troubled, and questing youngsters, often at times of particular stress. Lovely vacation and retreat spots appeal to disoriented and lonely people.

But why are there so many Jews among them? Nobody knows for sure. Some say that the Jewish community does not make enough of an effort to draw lonely young people close and that large synagogues lack a sense of warmth and intimacy. Some say that the permissiveness of many Jewish middle-class parents has left a vacuum of moral authority. Others say that the Jewish worship of reason and science has failed to satisfy a hunger for mysticism and emotion. Some say that Jewish concern with complex social and political issues has left young Jews unsatisfied and yearning for simple answers to life and purpose. Some say that our young people are starved for discipline, order, and obedience. Others say that the defection of so many of our children is an indictment of our Jewish educational systems and our Jewish family life.

For parents whose son or daughter is entrapped in such a cult, that is all very academic. After Guyana, nobody can be complacent about exotic cults. To parents, a child's conversion to a cult is not only a shock, a personal repudiation, a terrible failure; to most it is a heart-wrenching disaster. Such parents will go to any length to free their child from what they see as brainwashing, slavery, and spiritual death, and one of the most dramatic—and controversial—methods is *deprogramming*.

Deprogramming seeks to re-educate the cultist in a setting outside the cult's grip by conveying critical information about the group that the young person would otherwise never have a chance to absorb. This sometimes proves effective, particularly if the child goes home voluntarily and if the lines of parent-child communication have remained open. Usually a "knowledgeable stranger," preferably one who is an ex-cultist himself, can break through more easily than can the parents.

But what if the young person is unwilling to come home voluntarily? This is the dreaded dilemma faced by many parents. Do these parents then have a right to proceed with forcible abduction of their child in order to bring him or her to a neutral place for "deprogramming"?

Legally, there may be no such right. Children also have rights. Kidnapping is illegal, even if it is one's own child who is abducted. In addition, the terror which accompanies such abduction is often not conducive to the calm atmosphere necessary for re-education. Ted Patrick, the best known professional deprogrammer, and others have been judged guilty of criminal offenses for their involvement in kidnapping cultists at the request of their parents.

Legally wrong, yes, but is it morally wrong? If you were a parent who believed with all your heart that your child had been entrapped by an evil but charismatic leader into a cult which is wrecking the child emotionally and perhaps even physically, would you give up any device to save your child, even if it is illegal? No one can really understand the despair and desperation of these parents unless one has stood in their place. But, given these powerful emotions, is it morally right to use force in this situation? Is it an abuse of the child's privacy and conscience for the parent to resort to such methods? Would forcible abduction nullify the benefits of deprogramming? Should the Jewish community support the right of parents to resort to deprogramming, including—if necessary—forced abduction?

SHOULD GOVERNMENT STOP THEM?

The massacre at Guyana in November, 1978—together with the blood-curdling revelations of terror, sexual brutality, and brainwashing, culminating in mass suicide—shook the civilized world with shattering impact. Inevitably, shock and rage evoked demands to "do something" about the proliferation of cults throughout America and the world. This reaction was inevitable. If the US State Department had taken more seriously the information and protests it had received about what was going on in Jonestown, perhaps the massacre could have been prevented. And who knows what other horrors await a certain mix of circumstances in some other cult? Are we to sit by and let such monstrous barbarities befall our fellow Americans?

The reaction is understandable, but the dilemma is profound indeed. To "do something" translates itself inevitably into a demand for governmental action to restrict the operations of suspect religious groups. Holding the cults to complete obedience to all laws—including laws against guns, fraud, and financial exploitation—is necessary and proper. But in a land which rests on the principle of separation of church and state, what can and should government do in a situation like this? President Carter, in his press conference on December 1, 1978, said:

"I don't think that we ought to have an overreaction because of the Jonestown tragedy by injecting government into trying to control people's religious beliefs."

Similarly, the Justice Department, responding to severe pressure, said the government was wary about legislation to control such abuses because such laws might be "an infringement on the sect's free exercise of religion." Benjamin Civiletti, chief of the Department's Criminal Division, observed:

"Even if a sect requires its members to undergo long hours of work training and indoctrination with limited amount of food and sleep, it is questionable that these activities present a grave and immediate danger either to society or the members to warrant the imposition of federal criminal sanctions."

Civilleti cited several court cases, including a criminal prosecution of Hare Krishna in New York on charges that the sect falsely imprisoned members by "deception and intimidation." In dismissing the case, a state court had noted:

"Religious proselytizing and the recruitment of and maintenance of a belief through a strict regimen, meditation, chanting, self-denial, and the communication of other religious teachings cannot under our laws be construed as criminal in nature and serve as the basis for criminal indictment."

The court also said at that time that to sustain the indictment would "bring about a flood of unjustified investigations, accusations, and prosecutions and continue without end to the detriment of the citizens of our state and place in jeopardy our federal and state constitutions."

The dilemma is that the law cuts both ways. Freedom of worship for mainline religious groups also requires freedom for small exotic and bizarre sects. One person's religion is another person's sect. The sect of today can become a major faith group tomorrow. Then does this mean that a monster like Jim Jones can hide behind the First Amendment and work his evil under the protection of religious liberty? Not every evil can be cured by government. A vigilant press might have exposed Jonestown before the disaster struck. If conditions warrant it, restrained congressional investigations can also be helpful without impairing separation of church and state.

WHY NOT JEWISH MISSIONARIES?

When we Jews think of missionaries, we always think of others doing it to *us*. But, believe it or not, *we* used to do it to *others*. Indeed, 2,000 years ago, Judaism was widely known as a faith that sought converts. Nor was missionizing an unusual practice in Judaism. It was a classic Jewish position well documented in the Bible and the Talmud.

During biblical times, the ancient Hebrew tribes reached out to other people to bring them within the covenant Israel had made with God. The prophet Zachariah (8:23) envisioned the day when persons of every tongue would say to Jews, "Let us join for we have heard that God is with you." Nor was this only a dream; many strangers joined the Jewish people, among them Ruth, the Moabite-born wife of Boaz, who in our tradition is an ancestor of King David.

The Bible did not prescribe a formal procedure by which non-Jews could "attach themselves to the Lord," but in the days of the Second Temple, a formal system of conversion was established. Converts were then streaming to the Jewish fold. The victories of the Maccabees had stirred the Jewish imagination; inspired, they carried their religious enthusiasm to sympathetic Gentiles in Israel and throughout the Mediterranean world. It is said that, at the beginning of the Christian era, 10 percent of the Roman Empire, roughly 4,000,000 people, were Jewish. Conversions accounted for much of the increase in Jewish population in that period.

For centuries Jews proselytized Gentiles. Judaism never used professional missionaries; individual Jews were eager to share their knowledge of Judaism with others. Jewish missionary literature written in Greek still exists. Greek was the language then spoken everywhere in the eastern Mediterranean world.

Jewish missionary work came to an end when Christianity became the state religion of the Roman Empire under Constantine the Great in the fourth century. Harsh rules were enacted forbidding Jews to seek or even to *accept* converts. When these rules were ignored, the penalties for violation were made increasingly severe. Jewish proselytizing became a capital offense. Later, upon Islam's conquest of the Near East in the seventh century, Moslem rulers also used harsh measures to prevent Jews from converting others to their faith.

In the Middle Ages, Jews were often pushed and bribed to convert to the ruling faith. But converts to Judaism had much to lose, sometimes their lives. Even so, some cases of conversion to Judaism continued, including some high personalities in the Catholic Church. One of the most celebrated and colorful events was a mass conversion of the Khazars, in the year 740, when the pagan king of this obscure people, together with many of his nobles, embraced Judaism. This Jewish kingdom, located in what is now southeastern Russia, maintained its existence for several centuries, practicing toleration toward both Christianity and Islam, until it was finally crushed by a coalition of Russians and Byzantines.

Since the Middle Ages, Jews have continued to accept occasional converts, but clearly there grew a marked reluctance to accept them and revulsion against actively seeking them out. Why? We do not know. In America, with the steady growth of interfaith marriages, a growing number of people convert to Judaism every year, usually but not always in preparation for marriage. Courses for converts are conducted in New York City, Los Angeles, Boston, and several other communities. The evidence is clear that converts to Judaism, having made a positive *choice,* often become more actively engaged in synagogue and other aspects of Jewish life than do many born Jews—Jews by *chance.*

Then, why doesn't the Jewish community go out to more actively recruit converts?

There are good arguments on both sides. In favor of such a program is the mood of our times, in which millions of people feel estranged from the faith they were born to and are clearly searching for a meaningful faith to embrace. What faith could be more satisfying than one which is as old as recorded human history and which has provided the moral and spiritual basis for Western thought? Secondly, or to many *most* importantly, Jews are a shrinking population with no real possibility for expansion *without* large numbers of converts. Why should we act as if Judaism were an exclusive club, closed to all except those born into it?

Moreover, it is argued, why should Judaism be a religion for only white people? In a world in which a fast-growing majority is dark-skinned, why shouldn't a universal faith, grounded in social justice, seek out blacks, yellows, and all the races of humankind? There is yet another argument: additions of many persons of diverse racial and cultural backgrounds will enrich Judaism just as massive immigration to America benefitted American life. Born Jews would be strengthened in their own beliefs and faith if they had to enhance their own knowledge and appreciation of Judaism in order to communicate their faith to others.

Arguments abound the other way, too. The health of Judaism depends on the quality of Jewish life, not the number of adherents. Almost half of American Jews are presently not affiliated with synagogues or involved in Jewish life. We should concentrate on making Jews out of *them!* We must use our limited resources to build a worthy Jewish educational system at all levels rather than squandering our resources on a massive missionary effort which would cost vast sums and result in a small and dubious yield. Moreover, missionary efforts tend to become simplistic salesmanship; to reduce the grandeur of Judaism to the level of a TV commercial would be a terrible disservice to our unique heritage. We Jews are not just a religious group; we are a unique combination of people, faith, civilization, and nationality. Being fully Jewish is a matter of memory, of feeling, of a certain worldview, and even a special brand of humor. If a non-Jew wishes to join us, let him or her undertake a serious conversion and then join us. But let us not demean other faiths and cheapen ourselves by becoming salespersons of a Judaism reduced to a packaged commodity, available at bargain rate to every buyer!

Who is right? If the advocates of active Jewish proselytizing are right, how could we avoid the dangers suggested by the opponents?

In 1978, the UAHC Board of Trustees adopted a resolution, calling for a Jewish missionary program:

Rapid demographic changes affect the future of American Jewry. Some of these trends are: growth of mixed-marriage, a decline of the Jewish birthrate relative to the general populations, an increase in the number of non-Jews converting to Judaism. These developments require our serious and continuing attention. They call for creative leadership, so that we shape our future and do not become passive products of forces beyond our own control.

Accordingly, the Union of American Hebrew Congregations, resolves:

1. To intensify our formal and informal Jewish educational programs within the Reform movement to stimulate positive and knowledgeable Jewish identification.

2. To develop a sensitive program of welcoming and involving converts to Judaism, recognizing that those who choose Judaism in good faith are as authentic in their Jewish identity as those who are born Jewish.

3. To develop an effective program by which the Reform synagogue can seek out mixed married couples in order to respond to their particular emotional and social needs and to

make the congregation, the rabbi, and Judaism itself available to them and their families.

4. To plan special programs to bring the message of Judaism to any and all who wish to examine or embrace it. Judaism is not an exclusive club of born Jews; it is a universal faith with an ancient tradition which has deep resonance for people alive today.

"AND THE STRANGER WHO DWELLS AMONG YOU . . ."

By Lydia Kukoff, reprinted from *Compass,* Winter, 1978, a UAHC publication. Lydia is coordinator of the Post-Conversion Chavurah Pilot Project of the UAHC in Los Angeles, CA.

What do you do to become a Jew?

People who are interested in converting first attend classes in Jewish history, ethics, and customs. Following the course of study, some decide to convert to Judaism. These people go through a conversion ceremony and emerge, having cast their lot with that of the Jewish people, as full-fledged Jews.

Not quite . . .

Jewish law clearly states that the convert is to be regarded in all cases as equal to the born-Jew. In the eyes of the rabbis, the convert is like a newborn infant (Yevamot 48b)—an orphan who should be given an extra measure of love. The rabbis rightly realized that conversion is the washing away of former relationships and the birth of a new spiritual self. This newly adopted son/daughter of Avraham Avinu is a newborn child of the Jewish people. However, the very truth of this assumption emphasizes the disjunction which the new convert feels. There is a gap between the "baby" Jew and the adult human being which must be closed. In effect, converts are people with no past.

The classes which they attended were valuable as an initial step leading to conversion, but conversion is yet another beginning. Now that they have "taken refuge beneath the wings of the Lord," what happens when they emerge? It is not fair to expect that these "newborns" can know enough at this point to be comfortable with their new religion and its unfamiliar rituals.

I would suggest that one way to translate this "extra measure of love" into action is to create a support system to see these newest Jews through the often difficult transitional period following conversion. New converts often find that they have questions and problems which they are unable to resolve by themselves. They do not yet feel comfortable coming to the rabbi. Rabbis, sympathetic as they are to such problems, are busy with many other concerns and converts are likely to be very hesitant to intrude. Generally, there is no system for dealing with this situation. There is no one whose specific job it is to listen and to "be there" for these people.

By creating a support system, a chavurah for new converts (and spouses), which begins immediately upon conversion, the community is saying in a concrete way: "We care about you," "We want you to be a functioning Jew," "We want you to be part of us." Such a chavurah would begin at a time when these people are both receptive and full of feelings and questions not dealt with in the standard "intro" course, but which, in this framework, can be openly discussed. This does not mean that the chavurah is to be a group therapy session. Rather, it is to be thought of as a means to begin building a Jewish past on which to base a Jewish present and future. It would be an opportunity to explore the sanctification of time through the Shabbat, the holidays, and the events of the cycle.

Before each holiday, observances and customs would be discussed, demonstrated, and practiced so that each person would become familiar with them. Through the doing and through the support of the chavurah, members would gain valuable practical knowledge and new insight into Jewish values and traditions. They bind themselves to their new faith and they are given something to build on in future years. This chavurah is to be an intermediary step, an aid in acquiring a

Jewish identity and in encouraging a lifetime of fuller involvement. It is not intended to create a subculture ("convert") within the Jewish community, but, rather, to make of the convert a full enfranchised Jew, no longer a newborn but one well on the road to Jewish adulthood.

This idea of a converts' chavurah has long been a dream of mine. I converted fourteen years ago, after many months of learning and discussion with a rabbi. I was interested and involved in my class and eager to become a Jew. My conversion ceremony was one of the most beautiful moments of my life. Despite the fact that I had a supportive, knowledgeable husband and in-laws, my post-conversion exaltation was quickly replaced by feelings of confusion and ineptitude as I faced the realities of day-to-day life as a Jew. I felt stupid having to ask and unsure of myself. I assumed I was supposed to know since I had gone through conversion classes and I was a Jew. Eventually, I found friends who became models for me and I learned from them, but essentially I had to find my own path by trial and error.

I conceived the idea of the converts' chavurah because I am convinced that the distance from becoming to being can be positively, even joyfully, traversed. And, happily, so did the UAHC. This year, under its auspices, I will be setting up several chavurot in the Los Angeles area. We will meet one evening a week for eighteen weeks. In addition, there will be a camp weekend where we can share an intensive Shabbat experience. A network of support families, many of whom are converts, will be available so that chavurah members can have a place to spend Shabbat or a holiday and, incidentally, see that Jewish observance is do-able and joyful. They will see that by learning and doing one can be a full and equal Jew by choice as well as by birth.

Some might argue that there is no need for any of this. Aren't there, after all, many adult education programs and chavurot in the synagogues already? Yes, there are, but it is incorrect to assume that the majority of converts will join a synagogue immediately. Marriage is still the motivating factor in most, though certainly not all, decisions to convert. Often the Jewish background of the born-Jewish partner is minimal. The partner may have as much to learn as the convert. This couple may eventually join the synagogue when (and if) they have a child of school age, but how many years may stretch between conversion, marriage, and synagogue involvement? By then, the original enthusiasm felt at conversion may have faded during the years of disconnection. The answer to this problem, obviously, is to build on the naturally strong and positive feelings so evident at the time of conversion.

This, then, is a proposal to make of "your people," "my people." It is a reminder to the Jewish community. If converts are to be regarded as equals, they must be given the tools to insure that equality.

There should be no strangers dwelling among us.

6

SOVIET JEWRY

THE DILEMMAS LIVED BY SOVIET JEWS

Our lives owe so much to accidents of birth. If our parents had lived in Europe a generation ago, the likelihood is that they would not have survived the Holocaust. If we had been born in the Soviet Union, we would now be among three million Jews who live their lives in the peculiar limbo of a strange twilight existence. To the Soviet Jew, daily life is an endless dilemma. A brief look at the life of a Soviet Jew reveals the vivid contrast with the life of an American Jew. Perhaps a fictional portrait, but based on factual data, will help us not to take our own freedom for granted. . . .

You and your family live in a small, but pleasant, apartment in Moscow. Your father is an engineer and your mother works as a medical assistant at the hospital. Your sister goes to Moscow University, studying to be a doctor. Your grandfather, who is ailing, lives with you. It is somewhat crowded in the apartment, but your family is fortunate because you have a bathroom of your own, a refrigerator, and a television set. In most respects, your lives are much like your neighbors'. You, like many other teenagers in Moscow, love to listen to Western records, despite the disapproval of Communist party leaders. You go to poetry readings, especially to hear your favorite, Yevgeny Yevtushenko. You marvel that a non-Jew could have written the poem, "Babi Yar." (See the reprint at end of chapter.)

There is nothing distinctively Jewish in your home, except your grandfather. He is still religious, although he never prays in the house and performs none of the rituals of Orthodox Judaism in the apartment. You have never asked why, but you assume that your father has let it be known somewhere along the line that he doesn't want any trouble with the authorities. Your father, mother, sister, and you are all atheists. Your education is, of course, totally secular. There is no such thing as a Jewish religious school or Hebrew school. You doubt if you would go, in any case. Your grandfather goes every day to the Moscow synagogue, and, on the High Holy Days, the rest of the family sometimes joins him. Your father is always uncomfortable going to the synagogue. Once he whispered to you not to talk to anybody in the snyagogue, especially to American tourists and Israelis, because "there are spies planted in the synagogue." There are no Jewish organizations to which to belong—they are not permitted—but you don't think anything of this because this is the way it has always been. Your father occasionally speaks in Yiddish to your grandfather, especially when they don't want you kids to know what they're saying.

Mostly you don't think about being Jewish. Once in a while one of your classmates will make a nasty anti-Jewish crack, but it never bothers you too much. The day war broke in Israel, in 1973, was a strange moment in your home. Not one word about the war appeared the first day in *Pravda* or *Izvestia*. You heard about the war by listening to the short-wave radio picking up foreign broadcasts. It was so strange. You knew that your country was championing the Arab cause and denouncing the Israelis as imperialist, lackey aggressors. But you all sat down to the table and each of you knew that your hearts were trembling for the people of Israel. You wondered why. Your grandfather, frightened and excited by the war in the Middle East, began to talk nervously and for once your father did not cut him off.

Papa (which is your name for your grandfather) recalled his own childhood, growing up in a shtetl to which Jews were consigned in a little Russian town called Zhitomir. Jews were prevented by law from living in much of Russia's territory. It was the days of the Czar and of official and popular anti-Semitism and intermittent pogroms by wild and drunken Cossacks, but Papa painted a colorful and vibrant picture of the rich Jewish life, the intense education, and the strong culture which made the shabby shtetl so remarkable a place. Jews were barred from most professions and from government service; most Jews were very poor. He remembered the many friends who sought to escape military conscription and poverty by going to America. Oi, he mused, how he wished he had had the sense to join his cousins in their flight to America.

Then he recalled, in the 1910s, the upheaval of political turmoil, the ugly frame-up of Mendel Beiliss on a trumped-up blood-libel charge, and the riotous demonstrations of the revolutionaries. After sixty years, he was still able to recall in minute detail everything that happened to him in the stormy days of the Russian Revolution. He reminisced about his wild hope that the revolution would spell a new and better life for all Russians, including the Jews, who enjoyed first-class citizenship for the first time.

When he reached the rise of Stalin in his chronology, a peculiar thing happened. Involuntarily, he dropped his voice to a whisper. He ticked off the names of great Yiddish poets, writers, and playwrights who had been shot by Stalin's secret police in 1952. He named the Jewish theaters, the seminaries and Hebrew schools, and Yiddish clubs that had been closed down. He recalled his friends and relatives who had been banished to Siberia on such vague charges as "circulating Zionist literature" or "cosmopolitan thinking." He scoffed at the establishment of the Soviet Jewish province of Birobidjan, which the authorities never permitted to become "Jewish." He remembered the panic which spread among Jews throughout Russia in the 1950s, as rumors persisted that the entire Jewish community would be banished to camps in Siberia. Then, immediately before Stalin's death on March 5, 1953, the frightening "Doctors' Plot," in which the now old and deeply psychotic dictator, imagining that Jewish doctors had plotted against his life, prepared to wipe out his "enemies." After Stalin came Khrushchev whom Papa referred to as "the fat one." Said Papa: "He was, of course, also a no-good anti-Semite, but things were better, much better, than with Stalin." He described the new mood of Jews, no longer worried about violence or a knock on the door, but still not free to be Jewish.

Next morning your entire family went to the synagogue. You didn't go to pray. You wouldn't even know how to pray. Your real reason was the same one that drew so many others there that day—to get the news. Was Israel safe? Had the Arabs succeeded in destroying your brethren? Your heart was in your mouth. It was funny how the good, miraculous news seemed to course through the congregation like electricity. Nobody seemed to be speaking but everybody seemed to know. There was something about the happy tear in the eye of the old man, the smile, the strong handshake, the shoulders thrown back proudly. It was all right; you heaved a sigh of relief. But why did it mean so much to you? You weren't sure.

You could not explain it. You are Jewish. You feel Jewish. But you can't recite the prayers and you don't even believe in prayer or religion. But you like to be with other Jews. So you feel good when you go to the synagogue. When Yiddish actors occasionally perform, you go, though you know no Yiddish. Once a year, on Simchat Torah, you have an overwhelming need to show everyone that you're Jewish, so you join the throngs of young Jews who sing and dance outside the synagogue. Even your friend, Andrei, who is a leader of the Komsomol (Communist Youth), joins with you in these demonstrations. One year, there were 30,000 of you singing and dancing and crying. Andrei makes long speeches about the evil of Zionism and the reactionary character of the Jewish religion.

But you suspect he was as emotional as you were during the Israeli crisis. You didn't talk to him about it. It is better not to talk too much, especially not to party members.

Sometimes you feel that you would like to know more about your Jewish roots, but no Jewish schools are permitted and no opportunity to fill the void. You once asked your mother why it is that other nationalities in Russia have their own schools, newspapers, books, theaters, and cultural life, but Jews did not. She replied with a Russian aphorism which you didn't understand clearly but which suggests that they let us live but barely. Occasionally you take your grandfather's copy of the Yiddish newspaper, *Sovietish Heimland,* and struggle to make out a few of the Yiddish words, but grandfather always reproves you with the words, "Why break your teeth, my boy? It is nothing but government lies anyway." Father gets angry when he hears the old man talk to you that way. "Listen," he says, "I have a good job, a good apartment, a good life. Your babbling could take it all away. The boy wants to become a chemist, the girl a doctor. It will be hard enough without you." And always you feel bad for Papa when he is reproved in that way. He sulks a while and drowns his irritation in tea.

Why do you feel so Jewish when your Jewish life is so empty? Perhaps it is because the government insists upon identifying Jews as such, but then singles them out for special discrimination. Your parents, like all Jewish adults, have the word "Yevrei" on their identification papers which must be carried by all Soviet citizens. The government constantly proclaims that anti-Semitism is illegal and impossible in the Soviet Union, but you know that there are quotas in colleges and schools, that Jews are excluded from many sensitive positions in the party and government, and that Jews are identified publicly as Jews when they are arrested for so-called "economic crimes" (a capital offense in the Soviet Union). The handful of rabbis in the Soviet Union are not allowed to attend international conventions with their colleagues abroad; yet other religious and nationality groups in Russia have their own national associations and relate to their co-religionists abroad. The rabbis are very old; there is no one to replace them. What will happen when they die?

You sometimes wonder what it would be like to live in America. But is it really true that Blacks are enslaved and that the workers are beaten and degraded by the capitalist bosses and that anti-Semitism rules the nation? You also wonder about Israel. What would it be like to live in a Jewish state? Are the Israelis really agents for American imperialism? You cannot really believe these things because a government that can call Israelis Nazis will stop at nothing, but how can you know? How can you check? How can you determine the truth? What would it be like to live a fully Jewish life? More and more of your friends and their families are talking about emigrating. Would you want to? Papa often says that, in another generation or two, Jews will disappear in the Soviet Union. "They no longer kill us with pogroms," he says, "now they kill our souls by not letting us live as Jews." You wonder, sometimes, whether he is right, and it makes you rather sad. You don't know much about Jewish history, but you have heard something of how Jews suffered at the hands of the Hitlers of the ages and you know from Papa of the robust Jewish life and literature of Eastern Europe and it troubles you to think that the end of the road may be approaching for Jewry in the Soviet Union. What possibly could happen to change the situation . . . ?

And yet something *has* happened to change the situation. And that *something* is almost as *miraculous* as the exodus from Egypt in ancient days or, in this century, the restoration of the State of Israel. It is not that the Soviet Union has suddenly permitted its Jewish citizens to practice their Judaism and to live a full Jewish life in Russia. No. But what *has* happened is that Soviet Jews broke their silence. They began to speak out, to demonstrate, to protest, to *demand* the right to live *as* Jews—or to leave the Soviet Union. The growing Jewish spirit in Russia, within a few short years, led to thousands of underground Jewish study groups, Hebrew classes, places for discussion of life in Israel. Suddenly, thousands—hundreds of thousands—of Soviet Jews risked everything by going to the appropriate offices and *applying* for an exit visa to Israel.

Many were browbeaten; most lost their jobs instantly and were then hounded by the authorities as "parasites." Some Jews were harassed by the secret police, arrested, tried in "show trials," and sentenced to long prison terms. Some were "declared" to be crazy and were placed, involuntarily, in mental institutions.

But, despite these brutal Soviet tactics, the Jewish resistance movement inside Russia became invincible. What could the Soviets do with thousands upon thousands of Jews, mainly young, who insisted upon placing their lives on the line, willing to take any risk, demanding the right to be repatriated to what they insisted was their true homeland—Israel?

What happened astounded the world. The gates of Russia began to creak open. Almost 200,000 Jews left between 1971 and 1980. Why did the Soviets let them go? The first reason is the fierce determination of the Jews themselves. Unless Russia was prepared to sink once again to the bestiality of the Stalin period, or emulate the Hitler massacres, there was no way it could break the spirit of an aroused Jewish people. For the Soviet Union of today is not Russia under Stalin. Today the Soviets are acutely sensitive to world public opinion, particularly in the United States. The Russians need detente with America, particularly because of Soviet-Chinese tensions. The Russians want SALT, trade, technology. Soviet treatment of its Jews is a black mark on the Soviet reputation in the world. Moreover, the United Nations has declared that the right of a person to emigrate from his or her country of birth is a universal human right.

The Soviets want to hold themselves out to the world as champions of justice and freedom. Thus the gathering world-wide protests—from intellectuals and even from Communist parties in the West—profoundly embarrassed the Soviet Union. Jews throughout the world—and especially in the United States—have mobilized public opinion against Russia's policies toward its Jews. Thus far, world opinion has not led to significant concessions to Jewish rights *inside* Russia. But outraged world sentiment has burst open a door few people thought would ever open in our time.

Next only to the reemergence of the State of Israel into history after 2,000 years, the one event in recent time which struck many Jews as being almost miraculous was the mass exodus of Jews from the Soviet Union in the last decade. The iron gate was opened grudgingly, hesitantly, resentfully, but it was cracked open enough to let 1,000 Jews out the first year (1970), increasing to nearly 35,000 by 1973, dipping to approximately 13,000 in 1976, then rising in 1979 to an astounding 5,000 emigrants a month. In the chill of the American response to the Soviet invasion of Afghanistan in 1980, the numbers declined.

THE DROPOUTS

Today the drama of Soviet Jewry has taken a turn which has transformed the entire Soviet Jewry movement. The crisis is implicit in these startling figures: In 1970, more than 95 percent of those Soviet Jews who left the Soviet Union resettled in Israel. By 1980, more than 60 percent of the Jewish émigrés chose to resettle *not in Israel* but in the United States, Canada, and other Western countries.

This drastic reversal has generated a profound moral dilemma throughout the Jewish world—in Israel, in the Soviet Union, and in the United States. It has stirred intense controversy, raising the spectre of unhealthy divisions in what had been a united and effective campaign on behalf of Soviet Jewry.

What caused the sharp reversal? Expert opinions vary, but it seems certain that the aftershocks of the Yom Kippur War and the deteriorating economic picture in Israel shook up many Soviet olim (immigrants), and plenty of sabras, too, judging by the astounding number of Israelis ("yordim," meaning "to go down," a term of opprobrium) now living in New York City, Los Angeles, etc. Needless to say, cruel Soviet harassment, reaching new levels of severity, had its effects, and the Soviets turn the spigot off and on at their whim. In addition, although Israelis voluntarily reduce their own standard of living in order to share their limited resources with their Soviet brothers and sisters, the truth is that the difficult and time-consuming process of absorption in Israel alienates many Russian Jews.

For example, when Soviet Jews finally land at Lod Airport just outside of Tel Aviv, many after years of anguish since the moment they first applied for visas, they arrive bleary-eyed, tense, exhausted, and disoriented. Yet, at the terminal itself they are shuttled into lines for "processing," where Israeli officials confront them with forms which involve critical life decisions affecting their futures in Israel. Similar insensitivity in terms of housing, jobs, ulpanim (schools for learning Hebrew), and relations with the bureaucracy has often quickly chilled their ardor. It is known that these and many other complaints filter back to those still in Russia in streams of letters from Israel, and the dampening effect is not surprising.

Which raises another question: What are the *real* motives of Soviet Jews demanding emigration? That motivation must be intense; why else would they invite the harrowing obstacle course of social ostracism, deprivation of jobs, sometimes KGB harassment, and possibly even imprisonment, which an application can and often does evoke, and which all of these Jewish would-be emigrants knowingly and bravely endure.

Why? For some a form of Soviet Zionism, powerful and totally unexpected, does clearly operate. These Jews, like the chalutzim (pioneers) of Israel's early years, burn with a fierce Jewish spirit and will to live as Jews, sufficient to transcend the obstacles to emigration in Russia, and, later, the less harsh but still difficult adjustment in Israel.

But the others? Most Russian Jews are no more heroic than other men and women. They are ordinary people. What they have in common is that they want out of Russia. Some to live a full Jewish life; some to participate in the destiny of the Jewish people and the Jewish state. But many, perhaps most, just to get out of the Soviet prison to live a better life, to breathe some free air at last. For many of these people, Jewishness is a small consideration, if it is any factor at all. A better life abroad is the magnet. And for that, why select a war-shadowed, troubled, cruelly-taxed, tiny country in the Middle East if one can go to the "golden miracle" of America?

Then what is the crisis? Increasingly they come here and not there. The United States has generously welcomed Soviet Jews under special immigration provisions; the Soviet Jews are received and resettled by Jewish agencies.

To Israelis, the choice of America by Soviet Jews is not mere rejection; it is rank ingratitude and borders on betrayal of the Jewish people. Not only is it Israeli VISAS which made possible their liberation from Russia; it is ISRAEL which has opened its doors and its heart, and whose people have sacrificed deeply to accommodate the Russian olim. And it is ISRAEL—indeed, *only* Israel—which desperately needs Soviet Jews. Soviet Jewry is the only large reservoir of educated, technically and professionally trained Jews available for aliyah. Was it not for the ingathering of the exiles that the Jewish state was recreated? And now they desert Eretz Yisrael for the fleshpots of New York, San Francisco, and Vancouver rather than share in the rebuilding of a Jewish homeland. The disappointment and disillusionment with the "noshrim" (Hebrew for "dropouts," a term of contempt) are both deep and understandable.

But, lamentable as this may be to Israelis and to many Diaspora Jews, what can be done about it? Can anyone curtail the free choice of those who had the fortitude to resist Soviet tyranny? Can Soviet Jews be *compelled* to go first to Israel? Would that be a just, a Jewish solution?

Some leading Israelis—and some Jewish leaders in the Diaspora—have concluded that the time for a decision in this matter has come. They have argued that the current situation is intolerable. They recall that the basis for Soviet permission to leave is reunification with families in Israel. This so-called "repatriation" is the entire Soviet rationale for allowing Jews to emigrate; the Soviet Union has not simply flung open its doors for all Soviet citizens to leave. Any such universal right to emigrate would undermine the Soviet system. Millions of citizens would vote with their feet—and Soviet leaders show no inclination to preside at the liquidation of their empire.

Therefore, it is contended, if the current trend continues, the Soviet Union might simply repudiate the Soviet Jewry movement as a "fraud" and a "deception" and either reduce further emigration or cut it off entirely, placing responsibility for its end on Jews and on Israel. And even if this dire consequence did not occur, it is feared that the exit possibilities of Jews who DO wish to go to Israel will be reduced; that the current situation might undermine the validity of Israeli visas issued in Moscow; weaken political support for the public campaign on behalf of Soviet Jews and impair the morale of the activists within the Soviet Union.

One possible solution has been floated: Soviet Jews wishing to emigrate to the United States would apply *in* the Soviet Union for a visa to America. They would exercise their freedom of choice *in the Soviet Union,* rather than in Vienna as in the present situation. Upon arrival in Vienna, those with visas to Israel would be given resettlement help by the Jewish Agency to go ONLY to Israel. The others would be on their own.

This trial balloon set off a storm of controversy in the Jewish community. American Jewish leaders, as well as Israeli leaders such as Abba Eban, denounced the proposal. They charged that it would violate freedom of choice and restrict Jewish emigration. They argued that, much as we may wish Soviet Jews to choose Israel, the Jewish community would be abandoning its deepest religious and ethical principles if it turned its back on fellow Jews who choose to go elsewhere. They rejected the notion that Jewish organizations should deny assistance to any Jew coming out of the Soviet Union and requiring help to get to another destination. And some Jewish leaders decried the notion that American Jews, who have themselves not chosen aliyah, have the moral right to *impose* aliyah on Soviet Jews who placed their futures and their lives on the line to fight their way out. Moreover, opponents doubted that the Soviets would let significant numbers go to the United States in any event. They also doubted that the Soviets are about to slam the door to emigration and warned against tampering with the present arrangements.

In this grave moral issue, Diaspora Jewry—and especially United States Jewry—has asserted its independent judgment. Its dissent undoubtedly signifies a change in Israel-Diaspora relations—not a split but a new spirit of candor and mutuality. This spirit is in striking contrast to the reflexive and automatic reaction which almost invariably marked the response of Diaspora Jewry since the creation of the State of Israel. The emergence of a more difficult, but more mature, relationship between Israelis and American Jewry, based on unity in diversity and on mutual respect, can be discerned in the outcome of the painful "dropout" debate.

If any Israeli government should seek to limit the free choice of Soviet Jews, one can be sure it will not lightly disregard opposing viewpoints in the Jewish world, articulated eloquently by Abba Eban, former Israeli United Nations ambassador and foreign minister, who said, in part:

"Israelis and American Jews alike believe that Jews who emigrate from the Soviet Union to the United States with Israeli visas do great disservice to the central interests of the Jewish people. . . .

"Yet with all the severity of this judgment, I hope that American Jewish organizations will reject any advice to withhold aid and compassion from Soviet Jews who reach a free haven anywhere in the world. The deepest issues of Jewish fraternity are here at issue. Since our Jewish relationship is fraternal, it imposes an unconditional solidarity.

"Zionism has an absolute obligation to the interests of every Jew, in rectitude or in error, for better or for worse. The obligation is transcendent and all-embracing. It springs to our conscience from the depths of our tragic history. And it is sustained by memories too poignant to discard.

"Aliyah is a unique and translatable idea. But it is totally incompatible with any concept of coercion. If it lacks the voluntary impulse it becomes drained of its nobility. Nor is there much prospect of durability in a sojourn in Israel engendered by the pressure of deprivation imposed by a docile but reluctant American Jewish decision. The moral implication is intolerable.

"American Jews who have shown an infinitely smaller tendency toward aliyah than Soviet Jewry have no right to compel Soviet Jews to fulfill an obligation that American Jews largely ignore. Whatever the motives for the American Jewish record on aliyah, it must surely generate a decent humility toward Soviet Jews who are unable or unwilling to fulfill the dictates of our national history."

HUMAN RIGHTS

In addition to the difficult question of the noshrim (dropouts), a new challenge has emerged. President Carter has made the issue of human rights central to US foreign policy. The President challenged the Soviet regime to live up to its own commitments in the Helsinki Accord and at the United Nations to respect human rights, including the right to emigration. Thus far, the Soviet leadership has reacted angrily, charging President Carter with interference in the internal affairs of the Soviet Union and endangering detente. Some American observers have also been nervous about the effects of United States drum-beating on human rights, particularly since we do it so selectively.

For us, these events raise poignant new dilemmas. Is President Carter's well-meaning and noble campaign for human rights potentially hurtful to Soviet Jews? Most Jewish activists say "No," that it will help in the long run, but no one can be sure. Should we urge the President to mute his public criticism of the Soviets and to rely instead on "quiet diplomacy"? But we Jews have been burned many times by "quiet diplomacy"—President Roosevelt said he would try that route in seeking to help European Jewry threatened by the Nazis, and history records that shameful failure.

Also, many Soviet non-Jews are courageously standing up for human rights in the Soviet Union. Perhaps the best known—and most gallant—is Andrei Sakharov, inventor of the Soviet H-bomb and leading champion of human rights for all groups and individuals within the Soviet Union. Sakharov speaks boldly for the rights of Jews, although he is not Jewish. Shouldn't we Jews also raise our voices in his behalf and in behalf of other non-Jewish dissidents in Russia? Yet isn't there a difference between Jews who want merely to leave and dissidents who want to challenge and change the system from within? Are there any dangers to Soviet Jews if American Jews ally themselves too closely with the democratic reform movement in Russia? It certainly is a question worth pondering.

AN ACTION PROGRAM

Telegram Bank
GOAL: To create an effective, fast, and powerful weapon enabling us to respond to a given crisis without a moment's delay.

PROGRAM: Telegrams will be sent to appropriate Soviet and American leaders when Soviet Jews are faced with arrest, imminent arrest, or any other precarious situation, as well as to congressional representatives before crucial votes.

Every congregation will ask its congregants to volunteer to have X number of telegrams sent annually in their names and charged to their telephone numbers. (Six telegrams per year at an approximate cost of $3.00 per telegram would be an appropriate suggested contribution by congregational members. That would mean $18.00, and 18 is the number in Hebrew for "chai"—"life.")

Postcards, Postcards, and More Postcards

GOAL: To involve all congregants in the process of attempting to influence their representatives while making it as easy as possible for them to do just that.

PROGRAM: This program, like the Telegram Bank, is based on two theories. First, that most people are well-intentioned but not well-motivated. In other words, they'll do but not on their own initiative. Second, we should strive for conservation of energy in a cause that so drains us because of its incredible demands. Hence, minimum effort—maximum results.

Congregational organizations should reserve five minutes at every meeting, to write and *sign* postcards to specific American leaders asking their support for Soviet Jews (particularly for legislation). The postcards can be collected and mailed on the spot. (Prestamped cards should be used.) Within five minutes you can have 500 postcards sent to your representatives!

Sisterhood luncheons, special temple functions, board of trustees meetings, TYG meetings, social nights, etc., are all appropriate occasions to help Soviet Jews in this way.

A donation box should either be passed around at the time of the postcard writing, or be prominently displayed in the temple, to cover the postage.

Adopt-a-City

GOAL: To meet the increasing needs of Soviet Jews —particularly that of "protection"—through personal involvement in their struggle.

PROGRAM: Every UAHC region should be encouraged to adopt a Soviet city and the Jews therein—those whose struggle is for emigration and those whose struggle is for the restoration of cultural and religious rights. Adoption personalizes the struggle, strengthens our commitment, and "protects" the Soviet Jews. To the extent that a given Soviet Jew is made "famous," the Soviet government thinks twice about keeping him or her. This program is intended to make those Jews who wish to leave "famous" and, therefore, protected as a result of our adoption.

Adoption will consist of the following:

1. Letter writing to interested Soviet Jews.

2. Phone calls of support and inquiry to Soviet Jews on a regular basis.

3. Direct support to Soviet Jews in need of financial assistance through packages and bank drafts.

4. Active support on behalf of the Prisoners of Conscience.

5. Visits to Soviet Jews in the adopted city.

6. Maintaining contact with Soviet Jews once they arrive in Israel. Spiritual absorption is essential.

7. Adoption of Soviet Jewish colleagues on a one-to-one basis by specialized professionals within our congregations (e.g., chemical engineer, journalist, etc.).

Visiting the USSR

GOAL: To make Jews aware how they can help Soviet Jews if they visit the USSR.

PROGRAM: Jewish-oriented trips to the Soviet Union should be encouraged.

Local rabbis or UAHC Soviet Jewry chairpersons should try to find tourists, business groups, academicians, and others intending to visit the USSR and persuade them to use their trips to benefit the Soviet Jew.

Briefing material will be supplied by the UAHC Task Force. Potential travelers should understand the implications of taking a pleasure trip and the possibilities of helping Soviet Jews while they are in the USSR. The American Jewish Congress has also prepared a good briefing pamphlet for visitors.

Education

GOAL: To educate people about the plight of Soviet Jews that they might understand how and why they must help.

PROGRAM: The UAHC Department of Education has developed

materials on Soviet Jewry for religious schools and adult education programs that can be used even where no expert on the subject is available.

Every student in a UAHC congregation should be offered a course on Soviet Jewry between the ninth and twelfth grades.

Soviet Jewry should be taught through action programs. Students should participate in telephone calls, letter writing, community demonstrations, picket lines, etc., as part of the learning process.

Every congregational library should have basic Soviet Jewry materials on exhibit for the many people interested in independent study. Posters, Soviet Jewry signs, up-to-date bulletin boards should be displayed prominently inside and outside of every congregation.

UNDERGROUND!

(A simulation of the path of Soviet Jews from oppression to freedom. Created by the members of the National Board Institute of the National Federation of Temple Youth, Kutz Camp-Institute, Warwick, New York. From the monthly series program, "How About This," Vol. II, No. 2. Edited by Rabbi Daniel B. Syme.)

Introduction

This program aims at giving participants a sense of the fear, frustration, humiliation, and triumph of the Soviet Jew making his or her way to freedom. Participants are briefed by "undercover agents," harassed by fellow workers and the "Soviet Secret Police" (KGB), helped to "Vienna" by a series of friends and advisors, then taken to "Israel" for a celebration and party.

This program is designed for regions, large youth groups, or small youth groups with the assistance of the congregation. It requires fifteen to twenty leaders and involves up to fifty participants.

Background Material

The process of leaving the Soviet Union is long and complicated. Here is a partial description of what Jews must go through in order to emigrate:

1. You must receive a *vyzov,* or affidavit, from a relative abroad, inviting you to join him or her. Jewish emigration is allowed by the Soviet government on the principle of family reunion.

2. You go to the Soviet Office for Visas and Permits (called the OVIR) and fill out a form with information such as family, parents, dates of birth, place of work.

3. You start acquiring other forms of documentation. One of these is the *karakteristica,* an evaluation from your place of work, signed by a local trade union representative. Merely upon application many Soviet Jews find themselves demoted or fired, often in the form of public excommunication by colleagues.

Children in schools or universities also get *karakteristicas.* This is often followed by ridiculing from classmates, cessation of normal advancements, dismissal from universities, or being unable to graduate.

4. You need a document from the local housing committee in which all members of the family must sign the agreement to go. Parents, even adults, must sign approval whether or not they are going.

5. You then return to the local OVIR, pay a $45 filing fee, and wait up to six months, at which time you receive a yes or no answer. The answer is usually no for people in jobs considered sensitive or of ideological or military importance. People in these posts leave them for menial labor during the application period.

6. If you are fortunate you receive a *razrewenia,* a license from the Soviet government stating that you can leave the country. A race against time begins—You now have 10 to 25 days to obtain many other documents in order to leave. For example:

a. That you have resigned your job and returned the workbook that all Soviet citizens carry.

b. That you have returned the trade union book, military service book, and resigned from school or university rolls.

c. That you have left your apartment in proper condition. If not, you must repair it or leave money to do so.

d. That you paid $1,000 for each emigration family member, $550 for renunciation of citizenship, and $450 for a passport.

7. You then travel to Moscow to the Dutch embassy which represents Israel, where you undergo a triple check by Soviet officials. If all forms and documents are completed, you finally receive your passport.

8. Transit visas must be obtained from countries you pass through on your way to Vienna.

9. Packing cases must be bought from the government as well as customs permits for what is taken out.

10. You are allowed to take only $100 worth of goods. All extras and valuables must be left behind. You go through customs at borders. (A recent *Time* magazine article told of sable collars being ripped off coats and of stones taken off rings. Also, many had to go through embarrassing examinations for "secret documents.")

11. You finally arrive in Vienna and into the hands of the Jewish Agency.

However, if you miss your deadline, you're jobless, homeless, and out of school, and may not leave. You must begin again.

Preparing for the Program

The following nine areas are required for this simulation:

1. *Secret meeting place:* Dark room where all participants meet to begin the program. Leader required: one "briefer."

2. *Secret UJA office:* This room should have a banner reading "UJA," a desk and chair for the UJA official, and seats facing the desk for 5 "Soviet Jews." Sealed envelopes with *vyzov* typed on them should be in a box in front of the UJA

official. Have one for each person. Leader required: UJA official.

3. *Office of the boss:* Banner reading "Moscow Factory" should be strung across the room. "The boss" sits at a desk, flanked by two "workers." Participants should sit opposite the desk. The boss will need a *karakteristica* for each participant. This should be another blank envelope with the word *karakteristica* typed on it. We suggest that you use a different color envelope than that for the *vyzov*. Leaders required: one boss, two workers.

4. *The bank:* A long table with two chairs behind it will suffice for a bank. A banner reading "Moscow National Bank" should hang on the wall. The two "tellers" will require preprinted checks, half made out for $550 (renunciation of citizenship) and half for $450 (for a passport). Make more than enough; you'll probably lose a few. Leaders required: two tellers.

5. *The Dutch embassy:* Everyone goes *to* the Dutch embassy. Only those who were refused money at the bank (see "Procedures") go in. The others watch the procedure from the doorway. A banner reading "Dutch Embassy" should hang on the wall. The "Dutch ambassador" will require checks in the same denominations as those which the bank uses. The ambassador will need a desk. Participants sit opposite it. Leader required: Dutch ambassador.

6. *OVIR/KGB office:* A banner reading "OVIR Office" should hang from the wall. A "KGB agent," uniformed if possible, stands behind a desk. An aide, also uniformed if possible, sits and fills out forms. The OVIR clerks should have a box of "passports," one for each person. The KGB agents take the *vyzov*, the *karakteristica*, and the money before issuing the passport. Leaders required: one KGB agent, one aide.

7. *Waiting room:* The waiting room should be lit dimly, as bare as possible. Three or four leaders maintain absolute silence as the "Soviet Jews" wait for "freedom." Each group should wait at least five minutes here. Leaders required: three or four.

8. *Vienna absorption center:* This should be a brightly decorated room. A banner reading "Vienna Absorption Center" should hang on the wall. Slides of Israel may be projected on another wall using a carousel projector. Leader required: one absorption minister.

9. *Israel:* This is the end of the line. A banner reading "Israel" should hang over the doorway to this room, preferably a large social hall or recreation hall. This is a big party. You should have refreshments, Israeli music, decorations, and a "greeting committee" for the new arrivals. Leaders required: five greeting committee members.

Procedure

Step 1—The secret meeting place: Participants are assembled in the "secret meeting place" where a briefing is taking place. A leader stands up and gives the following speech:

"We all know why we are here. Right? I have gotten my passport and I know what you have to go through. It's not easy to get a passport because, as you know, they make things very hard for our people in *their* country. Now that you have decided to go to *our* country, this is how you begin. You must have a letter from a relative in Israel explaining that you will have a job and a place to stay when you get there. Don't worry if you know of no relatives in Israel. This is no problem. To get your letter you go to the UJA office. There are people here to help you find the office. All I ask of you is that you please stay seated and we will call you five at a time."

Then the first group leader takes five people and leads them to the first station, the UJA office. (When the first group has passed station 1, the next leader begins. . . .) No more than five in any one group!

Step 2—The UJA office: After the five participants are seated, the UJA official says:

"I suppose that *you* are here to obtain your affidavit for a visa. Your name please. *(Reply.)* Do you know if you have any relatives in Israel? *(Reply.)* Here is your letter. You must be careful with this letter, and keep it with you at all times. In addition to your letter from Israel which you must present to the OVIR office, you must also present a character reference which you must get from your supervisor at work. *Good Luck.*"

The official then looks through files and gets letters marked *vyzov* for each person. The group proceeds to step 3.

Step 3—Office of the boss: After the group is seated, the boss says:

"So you need a letter for the KGB, eh? I hesitate to ask what this is for. I would not like to think of such a hard working employee as you as a traitor and deceiver of *our* motherland and comrades. Well, come with me, we'll talk this over with your fellow workers."

(They receive a character reference marked *karacteristica* and then are harassed by fellow employees as they leave boss's office and proceed to the bank.)

Harassment from Employment

EACH: So you are leaving, well.
You cannot fool us.
Is this paradise not good enough for you Jews? You
are never satisfied.
Well, wait and see what you get for this.

ALL: Traitors, get out of here.
   (They leave.)

Step 4—The bank: Three people are directed to #1 teller's line and two to #2. One person in the first line is refused funds and told to go to line #2 for a loan. The "successful" withdrawers receive the following speech:

"Do you want to make a withdrawal? *(Reply.)* How much? *(Reply.)* Ah, so you need money for an exit visa? What is your name? *(Reply.) (The teller checks the records for the person's name.)* Here is your money."

Teller gives each person two checks, one for $550 and one

for $450. The one person who is refused is told: "I'm sorry, but our records show that you do not have the capital."

When the teller hears of the need for $1,000 he nods discreetly and directs the Jew to the Dutch embassy where money *may* be available.

Step 5—The Dutch embassy: The person in need of funds enters the ambassador's office while the rest of the group waits within hearing distance. The ambassador says to the one person who was turned away at the bank:

"Why are you here? *(Reply.)* Wait just a minute and I will see what we can do. These funds are from the United States, and you should thank God that we have them for you."

The person receives funds and all are led to the OVIR/KGB office. Note that the funds are to be the same two checks for $450 and $550 which the rest of the group received at the bank.

Step 6—The OVIR/KGB office: A KGB agent then says:

"Let me see if I can guess why you are here. You want to leave our paradise on earth, yes? Are we not good enough for you selfish Jews? You never seem to realize it when you have things good. I doubt that you realize what you are asking for by doing this, as you foolish people are gluttons for punishment. Give me your money and your papers and I will write you up your passports. Oh, by the way, I should just let you know that your jobs will be changed for the good of the people." *(Be sinister.)*

Step 7—The waiting room: A leader says:

"You are now in the waiting room to Vienna. You will be here for an indeterminate length of time. People have been here from three months to twelve years. You will remain quiet and seated."

Step 8—Vienna absorption center: A leader says:

"We here would like to welcome you to the Vienna absorption center. There is not a great deal that we can tell you now, except that you are very lucky to have made it to freedom. You are a small few of the very many like you. We know that it will take you a while to adjust to the freedom that you have never had, but now *your* life is *yours* to live as you please the rest of your life. There is no turning back. According to Israeli law, you are automatically an Israeli citizen because you are Jewish. Go to Israel. Work hard and enjoy life and help Israel and the rest of the world to free your fellow Jews. Transportation to Israel is now awaiting you." *(Slide show of Israel if possible.)*

Step 9—Israel: Participants are taken to "Israel" where a welcoming party awaits them. Actual transportation is optional. We used a van to drive them to Israel. But walking is fine.

BABI YAR

By Yevgeny Yevtushenko, translated from the Russian by Max Hayward. Babi Yar was the scene of a Nazi massacre of Russian Jews.

There are no memorials over Babi Yar—
The steep slope is the only gravestone.
I am afraid.
Today I am as old in years as the Jewish people.
It seems to me now that I am a Jew.
And now, crucified on the cross, I die
And to this very day I bear the marks of the nails.
It seems to me that I am Dreyfus.
The worthy citizenry denounces me and judges me.
I am behind prison bars.
I am trapped, hunted, spat upon, reviled!
And good ladies in dresses flounced with Brussels lace
Shrieking, poke umbrellas in my face.
It seems to me that I am a boy in Byelostok,
Blood flows and spreads across the floor.

Reeking of onion and vodka,
The leading lights of the saloon bar
Are on the rampage.
Kicked aside by a boot, I am helpless:
I plead with the pogrom thugs in vain.
To roars of "Beat the Yids, and save Russia"
A shopkeeper is beating up my mother.
O my Russian people!
I know that you are really international
But those with unclean hands
Have often loudly taken in vain
Your most pure name.
I know how good is my native land
And how vile it is that, without a quiver in their veins,
The anti-Semites styled themselves with pomp
"The union of the Russian people!"
It seems to me that I am Anne Frank,
As frail as a twig in April,
And I am full of love
And I have no need of empty phrases.
I want us to look at each other,
How little we can see or smell,
    —Neither the leaves on the trees nor the sky.
But we can do a lot.
We can tenderly embrace in a dark room.
Someone is coming? Don't be afraid—It is the noise of
    spring itself
Come to me, give me your lips.
Someone is forcing the door?
—No, it is the breaking up of the ice. . . .
Wild grasses rustle over Babi Yar.
The trees look down sternly, like judges.
Everything here shrieks silently
And, taking off my cap,
I feel how gradually I am turning grey.
And I myself am nothing but a silent shriek
Over the thousands of thousands buried in this place.

I am every old man who was shot here.
I am every boy who was shot here.
No part of me will ever forget any of this!
Let the "Internationale" ring out
When the last anti-Semite on earth is buried.
There is no Jewish blood in mine,
But I am hated by every anti-Semite as Jew,
And for this reason,
I am a true Russian!

NEXT YEAR IN JERUSALEM

These are the closing words of Anatoly Shcharansky before sentencing in a Moscow court, as drawn from notes taken by his brother:

In March and April, during interrogation, the chief investigators warned me that, in the position I have taken during investigation, and held to here in court, I would be threatened with execution by firing squad, or at least fifteen years. If I would agree to cooperate with the investigation for the purpose of destroying the Jewish emigration movement, they promised me early freedom and a quick reunion with my wife.

Five years ago, I submitted my application for exit to Israel. Now I'm further than ever from my dream. It would seem to me cause for regret. But it is absolutely otherwise. I am happy. I am happy that I lived honestly, in peace with my conscience. I never compromised my soul, even under the threat of death.

I am happy that I helped people, I am proud that I knew and worked with such honest, brave, and courageous people as Sakharov, Orlov, Ginzburg, who are carrying on the traditions of the Russian intelligentsia. I am fortunate to have been witness to the process of the liberation of Jews of the USSR.

I hope that the absurd accusation against me and the entire Jewish emigration movement will not hinder the liberation of my people. My near ones and friends know how I wanted to exchange activity in the emigration movement for a life with my wife, Avital, in Israel.

For more than two thousand years, the Jewish people, my people, have been dispersed. But wherever they are, wherever Jews are found, every year they have repeated, "Next year in Jerusalem." Now, when I am further than ever from my people, from Avital, facing many arduous years of imprisonment, I say, turning to my people, my Avital: Next year in Jerusalem.

Now I turn to you, the court, who were required to confirm a predetermined sentence: To you I have nothing to say.

7

ENERGY AND ENVIRONMENT

"I own one share in the corporate earth and I am uneasy about the management."   E.B. White

THE DIMENSIONS OF THE CRISIS

(Unless stated otherwise, the factual data in this section are from "Energy Dilemmas" by the League of Women Voters Education Fund, 1977.)

Even the most fervent environmentalist must face the awesome challenge of the energy crisis which now confronts us. In the words of Senator Henry Jackson: "The energy crisis is all pervasive. There is no aspect of our domestic and foreign policy that it fails to touch." Nevertheless, the urgency and gravity of the energy situation are still woefully underestimated. Polls continue to show that some 50 percent of the US population still does not believe that there is a genuine crisis. This is so even in the face of much expert testimony that devastating shortages will occur unless swift and effective measures are taken to curtail our present reckless level of consumption and to develop sources of renewable energy.

123

A major study on the subject, recently published by the Massachusetts Institute of Technology (MIT), entitled "Energy: Global Prospects 1985–2000," the work of scholars and experts from around the world who are members of the Workshop on Alternative Energy Strategies (WAES), concluded:

"World oil will run short sooner than most people realize. Unless appropriate remedies are applied soon, the demand for petroleum in the non-Communist world will probably overtake supplies around 1985 to 1995. That is the maximum time we have: thirteen years, give or take five. It might be less. Petroleum demand could exceed supply as early as 1983 if the OPEC countries maintain their present production ceilings because oil in the ground is more valuable to them than extra dollars they cannot use. We don't have much time to learn how to replace or decrease our dependence on the fuel that for three decades has fed the expansion of western living standards and the hopes of all nations for material betterment. Time is our most precious resource. It must be used as wisely as energy."

It is clear, then, that any solution to the energy crisis requires a major educational campaign to awaken the public to the realities ahead. Thus far, our governmental leaders have had only limited success in this task. The Jewish community, through its broad network of ties with business, labor, religious, academic, and other civic groups, can contribute greatly to this vital public education effort. Why is the energy crisis particularly important to Jews?

No issue confronting the nation rivals in complexity that of energy. In challenging the nation to adopt a comprehensive and coherent energy policy at long last, President Carter warned of the possible catastrophic economic, social, and political consequences that could threaten our free institutions, limit our diplomatic independence, curtail our standard of living, despoil our environment, and divide us internally by regions and classes, unless we take immediate drastic steps to avert it or mitigate its effects.

We have already witnessed the wrenching economic disloca-
tions of inflation, recession, unemployment, and vast balance
of payment deficits reaching $30 billion for the United States in
1978, largely caused by skyrocketing oil prices.

The dire social effects, felt most immediately by the poor, are
now being faced by the middle class in every aspect of daily
life. The implications of such social tension and conflict for
intergroup relations are ominous. We Jews have usually
suffered when social upheaval and instability seized society.

The long range political results of these developments are as
yet unclear. The global scope of the energy problem requires
an unprecedented degree of international cooperation. As the
United States becomes more and more dependent on imported
oil—mostly from Arab nations—we run the risk of mortgaging
our foreign policy and national independence to Arab blackmail. If so, Israel could be in mortal danger.

America has developed the world's most productive economy, thanks in large measure to the fact that we inherited a land
overflowing with cheap and easily available fossil fuels. But the
era of cheap, abundant fuels has passed. Our supplies of oil
and natural gas are dwindling; foreign sources are increasingly
expensive and politically risky. Our first real glimpse of the
crisis came in the oil embargo of 1973. Our fuel and light bills
doubled, but all except the poorest Americans learned to live
with it. The unusually severe winter of 1976–77, followed by the
removal of the Shah of Iran and the disruption of that oil supply,
brought on another crisis on the energy front, suggesting to
more thoughtful Americans that no quick solution is in sight and
that we face a long, bumpy, and costly trip for the rest of our
lives.

The realities should be clear. Within a few decades the
United States will have used up all domestic petroleum
deposits worth developing. In addition, the world oil supply and
price structure is in the hands of a ruthless cartel, the
Organization of Petroleum Exporting Countries (OPEC), which
drives price upward at will, threatening the survival of western
economies. Even if there were no OPEC, world demand for oil

is now so large and growing so rapidly that, within ten years, it will probably exceed productive capacity anyway. This all means that from now on we will have to pay dearly for oil and use less of it. And the dream of early substitute energy systems may be just that—an impossible dream; new substitutes are not likely to be cheaper than oil and they will take precious years to develop.

But all this is only part of the problem. Our American standard of living will decline. Ever since the industrial revolution, America's thirst for energy has been expanding. Growing population explains some of that growth, but not all. While our population expanded by 34 percent between 1950 and 1970, per capita energy consumption escalated by 46 percent! So by 1970, we were using over 25 percent more energy than we were consuming only 20 years earlier. If we continue in that wasteful manner, our annual use of energy will *double* again by 1990. Sky-rocketing prices have slowed the curve somewhat for now, but we are far from being out of the woods yet.

Today the United States, and the world, stand at an historic watershed. The path that served us so well in the past can lead only to disaster in the future. Aside from declining energy supplies, there is also hard evidence that the vast quantities of energy we have consumed in the past have exacted a heavy price on our health, our environment, and our possessions. There can no longer be any doubt that the United States must conserve energy and, at the same time, search for new energy sources which will probably take 20 to 50 years to develop. The traditional American idea that "more is better" may no longer work; it may, indeed, be causing degradation of our environment and reducing the quality of life.

Each step in the energy cycle emits vast quantities of wastes. In the past, not much thought was given how to get rid of these wastes. But now parts of the world are quickly reaching their limits. Air pollution and water pollution threaten the lives of millions. For example, some metals corrode almost a hundred times faster in the unhealthy air of some of our major cities than in places where air is still relatively pure. The

Environmental Protection Agency (EPA) estimated that in 1970 the cost of air pollution damage to health, property, and vegetation was $12.3 billion. Air quality in America is contaminated by many pollutants, most notably the poisons that pour out of our automobile exhausts.

The need for energy and the need to combat pollution are often in conflict, and our society will have to learn to make wise trade-offs. For example, it is clear that we will now have to rely more heavily on the domestic production of coal, of which we have vast supplies. But can we do this without strip-mining which, in the past, polluted more than 10,000 miles of rivers and streams in our coal-mining regions? And what of the human price of coal production? Coal mining is one of the world's most dangerous occupations. In 1971, an average of one person died and 60 people were hurt for each 3 million tons of coal produced. If, as experts predict, we will have to mine 20 billion tons of coal before the year 2000 and safety is not improved, then some 6,400 miners will die and some 400,000 will be injured. Even worse is the terrifying disease called black lung, which already afflicts some 100,000 miners. Moreover, some scientists warn that intensive coal production will cause serious climate changes within a century, warming the globe by 10 degrees Fahrenheit by the twenty-second century, possibly causing drastic disruption in food production, dangerously raising the sea level and lowering the productivity of the oceans. Every course we take has costs, penalties, disadvantages along with the benefits. We will need awesome wisdom to determine the best choices.

NUCLEAR POWER

No choices are more vexing than those we face in the matter of nuclear power. Many experts still have grave doubts about the safety of nuclear power stations. Others doubt the economic wisdom of investing heavily in this form of power, even if it is safe. Yet, we are already heavily involved, and many people believe that there is no solution to the energy crisis without some reliance on nuclear power in the future.

The future of nuclear power is heavily shadowed by the terrifying accident at the Three Mile Island nuclear power plant in 1979. The near-disaster in that Pennsylvania power plant turned the dream of cheap, unlimited, and safe atomic power into a haunting nightmare. The lives and health of thousands of people living near Three Mile were at stake during the accident. In the wake of that event, the whole future of nuclear power is now in question. Many individuals and political groups now oppose any expansion of nuclear power in the US.

Even before the crisis at Three Mile Island, the future of nuclear power was darkened by several developments:

1. A government committee created by President Carter announced that finding a technically safe and acceptable method of storing radioactive waste for thousands of years now seemed more difficult than the government had realized.

2. The Nuclear Regulatory Commission closed down five east coast plants because of possible deficiencies in the capacity of the plants to withstand an earthquake.

3. The same agency rejected a one-in-a-million estimate of the probability of a serious accident at a reactor, implying that existing experience was not extensive enough to justify earlier optimistic estimates. Previously suppressed reports indicated that Three Mile Island was not the first serious nuclear mishap.

4. A mounting fear that the increased use of nuclear power generators by nations all over the world will lead to the spread of nuclear weapons, adding to the chance of nuclear war.

There are now 70 licensed nuclear reactors in the US generating approximately 13 percent of the nation's electricity. Permits have been granted for 92 additional reactors. Whether and how fast these and other reactors will be built is now an open question. At the least, stringent safety precautions will certainly be imposed.

Advocates of nuclear energy say we have little choice but to expand our nuclear power complex to meet the growing demand for electricity. They insist that nuclear energy is safe and is less expensive than other fuels. Thus, New York State, prior to Three Mile Island, had announced plans to increase the percentage of nuclear generated power from 17 percent to 36 percent by 1992. The major change would be a shift away from oil, which now provides 44 percent of all electricity generated in the state; oil would drop to 32 percent in 1992. Coal, now 17 percent, would rise by 19 percent. After the accident at Three Mile Island, these plans were temporarily shelved.

Barry Commoner, chairman of the Scientists' Institute for Public Information, doubts that nuclear energy will prove to be cheaper than coal or oil, mostly because of the immense increase in capital costs in the first few years of a nuclear power plant. Commoner says that power companies do not care about such stupendous capital costs because they merely include these costs in the rates they charge consumers. Moreover, he believes that the companies are now downplaying the viability of solar energy to protect their own futures. The scientists also warn that no solution has yet been found to the terrible question of disposal of the waste from atomic power plants. Burying the waste, throwing it into the ocean, blasting it into outer space—all these have been considered, but the safety and practicality of any of these methods have yet to be established. The only existing commercial plant for reprocessing nuclear waste, the Nuclear Fuel Services facility at West Valley, New York, turned out to be a disaster. It is now being dismantled at staggering costs and some 690,000 gallons of radioactive liquid waste remains to be disposed. What state is likely to accept such a plague? Other scientists think the problem of disposal of nuclear waste will be solved within the next 20 years. This is only one of many uncertainties hanging over the future of nuclear energy. How can America proceed on so uncertain a course without at least solving the dangerous problem of waste-disposal first?

The energy choices are so difficult, because the risks are so critical. If we choose wrongly in our energy policies, we will also set regions of the country against each other in bitter divisions. A vivid example is the struggle which raged for 13 years over the small town of Kaiparowits, Utah. A power plant, comprising a 3,000 megawatt generating station and four underground coal mines, was to be developed there on federal land to supply electricity mainly to power-starved California. The project had the blessing of the governor of Utah and people living near the site felt it would bring jobs and that pollution problems could be controlled. However, environmentalists strongly opposed the project, charging that the 600-foot smokestacks would be visible for 60 miles, would damage the national parks, contaminate the environment with mercury, spread an odor of nitrogen acid, and in general harm the natural beauty and purity of the land, air, and water. Under the pressure of the environmentalists, the proposed project was abandoned. Was that good or bad for America? What about the power needs of Californians? The goals of energy and ecology seemed in this clash to be on a collision course. It is clear that exclusive attention to one goal without a careful balancing of the others can be the undoing of America. Fanaticism, even for a noble cause, will not get us out of the dreadful bind. Sometimes "the best is the enemy of the good."

It will take careful judgment, common sense, a balanced weighing of conflicting values, and a capacity for fair compromise to get us onto safe ground once again.

All this presumes that there really is an energy crisis in America and the world. Many people, including some authorities, believe that the so-called "energy crisis" is a myth contrived and perpetuated by the oil cartel here and abroad to sweeten their profits for decades to come. These people say that, far from an existing energy shortage, the world is awash with oil; that this glut will increase as huge new reserves in Mexico, offshore China, South America, and elsewhere are developed; that multinational oil cartels have no loyalty to their own countries or to any international economic order but only to extracting the biggest profit possible per barrel of oil.

In this view, the United States government should bend its efforts to:

1. undermine the grip of the OPEC cartel,
2. enforce competition among the major oil companies,
3. encourage mandatory conservation,
4. stimulate creative development of solar energy and other sources of energy.

Many informed observers reject the Administration's grim energy scenario for the 1980s. "I'm sick of hearing that!" cried William Winpisinger, president of the Machinists Union, who opposed the Administration's energy program. "There isn't a scrap of evidence that will support it." Many critics argue that a policy based on expectations of scarcity is a "self-fulfilling prophecy" because new supply sources will not be considered under such circumstances.

One alternative to a policy based on shortages is a policy of oil proliferation. Instead of passively awaiting the dwindling of fossil fuels, why not anticipate the problem by a crash program of drilling in parts of the world that have not yet been explored? Advocates of "oil proliferation" argue that we do not know how much oil is really available in the world because we have done little drilling in most parts of the world. For example, a US Energy Department official conceded that more wells have been drilled in the state of Kansas alone than in all of South America. An Interior Department Oil expert—Bernardo Gossling—claims there may be three times more recoverable oil in the world than presently believed. Similarly, the World Bank estimates that some 60 developing countries have oil and gas potential, of which only 14 are presently producing. Mexico alone may have more oil in reserve than does Saudi Arabia.

Advocates of oil proliferation acknowledge that foreign oil will increasingly account for larger proportion of domestic consumption. That being so, they argue, why not increase supply sources to make the West less vulnerable to oil blackmail by a handful of OPEC countries? Uncertainty about new supplies might very well stimulate restraint in the oil cartel's pricing decisions.

At this point little progress is being made in any of these

directions, but hard decisions await us in the face of ever-higher prices exacted by OPEC countries, which threaten the very existence of the West.

But, we cannot solve the energy crisis without taking into account the need to protect the integrity of the environment. How to balance these vital, and sometimes conflicting, values will test our wisdom in the decades ahead.

STATEMENT ON ENERGY CONSERVATION BY THE SYNAGOGUE COUNCIL OF AMERICA

Purpose

Since the oil embargo of 1973, Americans have become painfully aware that, not only our energy supplies, but our economic well-being and the soundness of American foreign policy have been deeply affected by our dependence on foreign oil. We have become more conscious of our thoughtless use of precious, non-renewable resources at the expense of future generations. The deeply rooted Jewish ethic forbidding "wanton wastefulness" becomes freshly evident to us as American Jews. We are faced with the necessity to consider whether our continued personal satisfaction requires the level of consumption to which we have become accustomed, or should we relearn the principle of being "rich" with our "portion," regardless of its size.

In economic terms, the consequences are obvious. During the past six years, OPEC and the oil companies have been able to:

1. create a substantial US balance of payments deficit of $28 billion in 1978 alone,

2. jeopardize the value of the dollar in overseas money markets,

3. contribute substantially to US inflation.

This dramatic economic effect has had a further impact. The

American government is finding itself increasingly unable to fund the social and economic programs which the Jewish community has traditionally endorsed.

All of this confirms the need for the United States to achieve energy independence. The American Jewish community has special cause to be actively involved in the effort to help the US government to achieve its goal. Only independence can assure a sound US economic and social fabric at home and an independent foreign policy abroad. It must be the special obligation of the synagogue to educate and inform the people of the true nature of the energy problem and to develop practical programs for synagogues as well as homes. The Synagogue Council of America presents the following series of proposals.

Conservation

There is no easier, more immediate way for the American Jewish community to deal with the energy crisis and to help the United States move toward energy independence than by reducing consumption. The Synagogue Council of America (SCA) believes that current patterns of consumption by Jewish organizations and individual American Jews are wasteful and contrary to religious values.

To assist Jewish organizations, the SCA has prepared a series of minimal steps that it recommends be implemented as soon as possible.

I. CONSTRUCTION AND PLANT UTILIZATION

A. General

1. Every synagogue should conduct an energy audit.

2. No synagogue should undertake construction or repair, without evaluating the amount of energy to be used.

3. Synagogues should encourage the use of facilities by other Jewish organizations to enable the Jewish community to reduce its overall energy consumption.

B. Insulation

1. Windows should be caulked and weather-stripped.

2. To reduce window heat loss, double glazing should be used; broken glass replaced at once.

3. Hot water pipes and heaters should be insulated.

C. Lighting

1. Fluorescent lights, four times as efficient as incandescent, should be used wherever feasible.

2. Outdoor lighting should be restricted to safety requirements.

D. Outdoor building exposure

1. Barrier walls should be built and plantings on northern and western sides should be installed to modify the effect of windy exposures.

2. Trees should be planted to provide needed shade in summer.

II. HEATING AND COOLING

A. Buildings should be equipped with separate automatic devices for each area of the building to control heat, light, and power to permit shut-off when not in use.

B. Heating thermostats should be set at 65°; cooling thermostats at 80°.

C. Facilities should be more energy intensive.

1. Schedule activities so that the building is closed one night a week.

2. All programs should be scheduled to provide most economic use of facilities.

3. Synagogue programs and meetings should be moved to private homes, whenever feasible.

D. Solar heating should be investigated.

E. Assure furnace efficiency through regular maintenance.

III. OPERATIONS

A. Appoint a synagogue committee to study the energy problem.

B. Arrange for car pooling, whenever feasible, to daily services.

C. Congregants should be urged to drive energy efficient vehicles, reduce home energy consumption, and insulate homes.

IV. PROGRAMS

A. Make the community aware of energy waste and consumption.

  1. Arrange discussion groups and lectures.

  2. Organize demonstration projects and workshops.

B. Make current information regularly available.

C. Call and write to local and national elected officials for support, in opposition, or in questioning decisions.

JUDAISM, ECOLOGY, AND THE ENVIRONMENT

"Michigan, Lake. Memorial services for Lake Michigan will not be held as such; however, visitation will remain in effect indefinitely. The lake, aged 23,031, died recently after many years of abuse, stemming primarily from pollution. The lake, once a popular sports and recreation area for millions of people, is survived by Lakes Superior and Huron. Lake Michigan was preceded in death by Lakes Erie and Ontario."

This mock obituary notice, written by David M. King, a student at the University of Illinois, reflects the powerful surge of concern, especially among the young, about the degradation of the environment in America—and, indeed, throughout the planet Earth. What we face today, it is now clear, is not merely another crisis. It is the stark question of survival. In Deuteronomy, God enjoins man: "See, I have placed before you the blessing and the curse, life and death. Therefore, choose life—choose life and live." Whether we, in our generation, have the will to choose life will determine the destiny of the human race.

Concern for the environment is not new. The prophet Jeremiah (2:7) could have been speaking to us when he warned his contemporaries: "And I brought you into a land of fruitful fields to eat the fruit thereof and the good thereof; but when you entered, you defiled My land and made My heritage an abomination."

Everyone who reads—or even looks around—can see how

badly we, in our time, have defiled the land and ravaged God's earth.

In California, pollution has created 50 percent more nitrogen acid in the air than ever before. Nitrogen acid filters light out of the atmosphere. If pollution escalates, California could receive no sunlight whatsoever.

Lake Erie, which once sported lovely swimming beaches and was a place of beauty, is so polluted there is fear that it might catch fire. It has been killed by the flood of pickling acids from the giant steel works which line its shores and from the torrents of sewage and detergents poured into it by the millions of people who live nearby. It has been estimated that the cost of cleaning up the disaster would be 40 billion dollars; and, provided all pollution is stopped, it would take 50 to 500 years to bring the lake back to life.

Oil drilling rigs working off the coast of Santa Barbara, California, vented tons of oil onto Santa Barbara's once spectacular beaches, causing immense damage to the beach and to the fish and wild life in the area as well as to fragile marine ecosystems.

More than 140 million tons of smoke and noxious fumes are belched into the air over the United States in one year, while 7 million automobiles are discarded along with 20 million tons of paper and paper boxes, 48 billion cans, 26 billion bottles and jars, 3 billion tons of rock and mill tailings, and 50 trillion tons of hot water bearing various kinds of acids and muck, in industrial wastes.

Hundreds of lakes, including many of the loveliest Adirondack lakes, are being destroyed—fish life has already died—because of acid rains, caused by the chemicals released into the air by power companies.

Skyrocketing population growth, together with technological growth, will doom millions to starvation and famine throughout the world. The population of the world is now over 4 billion; unless drastic population curbs are made, it will double by the end of the century. Ecology poses the deep religious, theological, and moral questions: What are we? Are we inherently greedy? What is our relationship to nature? Has God endowed us with dominion over nature? Is competition or cooperation the nature of our relationship to one another? What does it mean to be human? How can human life be made precious once again in an age of onrushing technology and crushing population pressures?

It has sometimes been charged that "the despoiling of the world about us is rooted in the Judeo-Christian ethic that views the world put here for humanity's benefit and enjoyment, an extension of the Garden of Eden theme." What these critics have in mind is the statement in Genesis: "Be fruitful and multiply and populate the earth and conquer her. Rule over the fish of the sea and the birds of the heavens and over all living things on earth. I have given you all the grass and trees for you and all other living things to eat."

A group of Protestant theologians have declared (*The New York Times,* May 1, 1970) that Christianity has contributed heavily to the current environmental crisis, asserting that solution of the problem of pollution would require change in religious values. The theologians said that the value of large families was one value that must be reconsidered. Another value in question was the value of a constantly expanding economy; another was the supremacy of human life over the rest of nature. The scholars said Christian thinking had sanctioned the exploitation of the environment by science and technology. They cited the biblical commandment in Genesis 1:28 as encouraging humanity to be indifferent to "the feelings of natural objects" and creating a gulf between people and nature. The Christian emphasis on individualism rather than society plus the preoccupation with the next world rather than this one were also criticized by the theologians as contributing to a climate in which economic ruthlessness was condoned.

Jewish tradition makes it clear that our "dominion" over nature does not include a license to slaughter indiscriminately or to abuse the environment. "You shall not destroy" is the basis of the talmudic law which prohibits willful destruction of natural resources, or any kind of vandalism, even if the act is committed by the owners of the property themselves. One must not destroy anything that may be useful to others. "The earth is the Lord's and the fullness thereof" implies that we are the stewards of nature, obliged to cherish and to preserve it. "You shall not see your brother's ox or his sheep driven away and hide yourself from them. If you see your enemy's ox going astray, bring him back." (Exodus 23:4) "If the donkey of someone who hates you is lying under its burden, you shall rescue it." (Exodus 23:50) "When you besiege a city, you shall not destroy the trees by wielding an axe against them, for is the tree of the field a man that it should be besieged?" The latter injunction alone is enough to condemn the defoliation policies we pursued in Vietnam, as well as the rape of the Redwoods in California and our forests throughout the United States.

The rabbis who followed the biblical period emphasized the Jewish traditional view:

"Woe to the man who stands on the earth and does not see what he sees, for in every drop of water in the sea and every grain of dust in the earth have I created its own image. . . . Of everything God created nothing was created in vain, not even the things you may think unnecessary, such as spiders, frogs, or snakes. . . . Man was not created until the sixth day so that if his pride should govern him it could be said to him, 'Even the tiniest flea preceded you in creation.' . . . Why did God appear to Moses in the lowly bush? To teach us that nothing in creation is without God's holy presence, not even the commonest bush. . . . When God created man He showed him everything in the Garden of Eden and said to him: 'See My work, how good it is. Know that everything which I have created, I have created for you. And now take care, lest you spoil and destroy My world. For if you spoil and destroy it, no one will rebuild it after you.' "

Jewish tradition does not accept unbridled individualism. The concept of the survival of the fittest has no sanction in the Hebrew Bible. Responsibility for the poor, the widows, the orphans, and the sick was the obligation of the total society, the community. No person could simply pile up wealth at the expense of everyone else. Every person had to leave part of the field for the use of the stranger. The field itself was to be spared from the planting every seventh year. The greedy were held in contempt: "Woe unto them that join house to house, that lay field to field, till there be no room, and you be made to dwell alone in the midst of the land!" (Isaiah 5:8) " 'The spoil of the poor is in your houses; what mean you that you crush My people, and grind the face of the poor?" says the Lord, the God of Hosts." (Isaiah 3:14–15) Fair weights and measures were regulated by the community. And while the Garden of Eden tradition puts human beings at the pinnacle of creation, people and nature are cherished together: "The heavens declare the glory of Gcd and the firmament shows His handiwork." Judaism has never seen people separate and apart from nature, as the licensed plunderer of a planet; Judaism calls on us to cherish and revere all that has been created in sacredness. In Jewish tradition, we and the world are one, inseparable and inviolable. Human beings and their world are both good and dependent upon each other.

God rules over nature and humanity, the two are interdependent, and God uses the environment to convey His message and to work His will:

The voice of the Lord breaks the cedars,
The Lord breaks the cedars of Lebanon.
The voice of the Lord makes the oaks to whirl,
    strips the forests bare;
And in His temple all cry, "Glory!" (Psalm 29)

Praise the Lord.
Praise Him, sun and moon, praise Him, all you
    shining stars!
Praise Him, you highest heavens and you waters
    above the heavens!
Mountains and all hills, fruit trees and all cedars!

Beast and all cattle, creeping things and flying birds!
Kings of the earth and all peoples, princes and all
    rulers of the earth!
Young men and maidens together, old men and
    children. (Psalm 148)

It will not be easy to reverse the ecological tide, especially in the light of the energy crunch. It will cost money—lots of it; some experts say a minimum of $25 billion a year for an indefinite period. But money alone will not assure success. Saving our environment and our energy will require truly revolutionary changes in our economy, our culture, our values, and our life style. The degree of management and control of the economy necessary to do both might well be inconsistent with American capitalism as we have known it. Pollution and waste are not simply the bitter fruit of capitalism—the Soviet Union and almost all industrialized nations face similar problems —but unbridled greed, masquerading as free enterprise, makes rational control impossible.

This national effort will focus our attention on the nature of human beings themselves. Must we accept a dog-eat-dog philosophy, cut-throat competition, as our highest way of life? If, as Archibald MacLeish tells us, all of us are riders together on one small planet, can't we find ways of building cooperation and community? The socialist experiment in the Soviet Union has been a dismal failure, but what morality sanctifies the right of a private entrepreneur to own a stretch of ocean beach on an American shore, a resource which should be the birthright of all, or to pour tons of industrial wastes from his factory into a river which is the lifeblood of all the residents of the city?

And the ecological crisis may compel us to examine our divinities. The real god in the world today—and nowhere more than in America—is technology. We have nourished the belief that technology can solve all our human problems. We had absolute faith in technology. But technology for what? The president of the American Public Health Association says we are "standing knee-deep in refuse, shooting rockets to the moon." What are the human goals we have lost in the smoggy haze of our industrial triumphs? We now know that technology, not clearly harnessed to meaningful social goals, can destroy us. We now know that endless economic growth, like endless population growth, is dangerous. We now begin to suspect that the production and consumption of goods are not the highest goals of human life. We now begin to suspect that excessive *quantity* can cheapen the *quality* of human life. The Gross National Product says nothing about the quality of life. We now begin to suspect that the solution of the problem may require a drastic reordering of our own individual life styles. Must a family have gas-guzzling automobiles? Should we consider banning the private automobile altogether—the great contemporary heresy—and build a mass transit system worthy of human beings? Will we have to adjust our standard of living toward more simplicity, as some young rebels have urged? How long can the world go on while the wealthy get wealthier and the poor get poorer? Can pollution be stopped without a redistribution of wealth and resources, particularly when we acknowledge that we Americans—6 percent of the population—use 50 percent of the earth's nonreplaceable resources and account for half the world's industrial pollution? Will we have to discourage large families, encouraging birth control and therapeutic abortions and eliminating income tax allowances for more than two children?

It may be that the environmental crisis can bring us together again. The world is truly one—we all sink or swim in the same battered planet. James Fenimore Cooper said long ago in *The Prairie:*

"The air, the water, and the ground are free gifts to man and no one has the power to portion them out in parcels. Man must drink and breathe and walk and, therefore, each man has a right to his fair share of each."

Overcoming the ecological disaster will compel us to radical (meaning going to the roots) and religious (meaning spiritual and moral values) changes. We will have to learn once again to value human life, to care, to share with each other, to work together, to renew our faith in humanity's capacity and in God's providence. We have worshipped long enough at the altar of consumption of goods and services; now we must, in order to survive, establish that fellowship among the peoples of the world, for which Judaism spoke at the beginnings of history. We must, in the ancient divine admonition, "choose life—and live."

8

ANTI-SEMITISM

If there is one thing on which we Jews are the world's foremost experts, it must be anti-Semitism. We are summa cum laude in the college of bitter experience. We have seen the evil of anti-Semitism masquerading as religion, science, politics, literature, even humor, in a hundred lands. We have seen its endless varieties, from the behind-the-hand bigotry of polite society to the death camps of Nazi Europe. So, if there is any subject we really understand, it is anti-Semitism.

The truth is that we do not understand the *causes* of anti-Semitism and we have nothing but vague suppositions about how to solve it. The only thing we are sure of is that we Jews can do nothing about it, only non-Jews can, even though its ebb and flow determines our life or death. Still we maintain large defense agencies to protect us against anti-Semitism, knowing in our hearts that they are only a form of weather forecasting to predict the shape of the storms without any real capacity to affect the weather.

President Anwar Sadat of Egypt was the first Arab leader in history to extend a hand of peace to Israel, although at one point in his life he was pro-Nazi and he showed signs of a primitive anti-Semitism even as he stood in Jerusalem.

143

In recent years, a surprising alliance has emerged between fundamentalist evangelical Christians and Jews. Why? Because their literal interpretation of God's words in Scripture made them fervent supporters of Israel at a time when liberal Christian groups seemed immobilized by doubt and uncertainty about Israeli policies. But the same literalness which predisposed fundamentalists to the Holy Land predisposed them also to contempt for Jews as "rejectors of the Messiah."

So who are our friends? Who are our enemies?

ARE JEWS RESPONSIBLE FOR ANTI-SEMITISM?

We categorically reject the notion that Jewish behavior causes anti-Semitism. It was not Jewish behavior, but Nazi policy and crimes, which condemned six million Jews to slaughter. Hitler claimed it was the behavior of Jews which made it necessary to eliminate them. They were capitalists; they were Communists; they owned all the wealth; they were an inferior breed; they were anti-Christ. But, if the bloody chronicle of anti-Semitism proves anything, it is that "good behavior" does not insure Jews against blood libel accusations, against religious persecution, against the dark fantasies of the rabble-rousers, against being used as scapegoats by cynical rulers. Anti-Semitism is a disturbance in the mind of the non-Jew. In Poland, shortly after World War II, anti-Semitism was fanned to a white heat to meet the evil purposes of government hate-mongers *even when there were hardly any Jews left in the land.*

But can it be that Jewish behavior does not have some effect on anti-Semitic attitudes? In the 1950s, at the height of the Cold War, Ethel and Julius Rosenberg were convicted and executed for betraying atomic secrets to the Russians. Certainly so terrifying a crime against America committed by a communist Jewish couple would excite anti-Jewish emotions in the public. Studies at the time found that it did not; most Americans were not even conscious of the Jewish identity of the pair. In the McCarthy era, when so many Jews were hauled before the Wisconsin demagogue and pilloried as betrayers of

America, many Jews shuddered at what they were certain would be the devastating impact on public opinion. Were they right? Studies allayed that fear, too. Later, during the Vietnam War, when public emotions were at their highest point, there were dire warnings of an inevitable backlash against the protestors; a vengeful public would remember the "Eisendraths, Lowensteins, and Abzugs," prominent Jews who were among the many outspoken leaders of the anti-Vietnam campaign, and settle accounts when the war's nightmare finally ended. It never happened.

In 1973, when Arabs clamped the devastating oil embargo on the West as a reprisal against Israel's "aggression," the same tune was heard; the American people, angry and irritated by the hassles of long lines and jacked-up gas prices at the pump, would look about for somebody to blame. Was there a more available scapegoat than American Jews, vocal advocates of Israel's cause? Again the American people defied the predictions. Instead they blamed the Arab sheiks for putting a gun to America's head, the oil companies for ripping us off, and the Administration for its inept response to the Arab assault on our economic life.

And now the same drama is unfolding, with a new cast of characters. The effort to gain peace in the Middle East has led to intermittent periods of bitterness in the relations between Israel and the United States. The Administration—and a growing segment of the public—blames Israel for "intransigence" in responding to peace initiatives. The media portrays Israel as preferring land to peace. In the background looms the spectre of another Middle East War—and perhaps another oil embargo. American Jews, caught in the middle, defend Israel, criticize Arab demands, and frequently attack the US government for its one-sided pressures on Israel. Tensions escalate. Public support for Israel seems to erode. Angry charges reverberate.

In such an atmosphere, can we be sure that, as in the previous cases, Jewish behavior will not significantly affect the nature and extent of anti-Semitism? Are there aspects of the

Middle East situation such as the energy crisis which make Jews specially vulnerable and are more dangerous than the earlier examples? If so, what restraints should guide American Jewish conduct to limit the damage to American opinion? If American public opinion turns against Israel, can we assume that this constitutes a rise in anti-Semitic feeling?

The Israel situation may be a new and special case, but in general we repudiate the notion that as a community Jews are responsible for the conduct of a particular person or group who happen to be Jewish. A nursing home operator who also happened to be an Orthodox rabbi was sent to prison in New York City for defrauding the government and the elderly patients in his nursing homes. If such an event, magnified by the media, stimulates anti-Semitism, should the Jewish community dissociate itself from such a person? If the Jewish Defense League (JDL) shoots up the Russian embassy and roughs up its employees, should we denounce them? It is a dilemma. But we are no more responsible for these hoodlums than the Italian community is for the Mafia or Blacks for notorious Black drug pushers or muggers.

THE IMAGE OF THE JEW

Is anti-Semitism influenced by the Jew as portrayed in literature, movies, stage, and television? We cannot be certain.

Whatever the answer, Jews are frequently portrayed in negative terms as grasping, greedy, super-ambitious, vulgar, and immoral. Jews read and watch such an image with revulsion and fear, as if looking over their shoulders to see how such a negative portrait affects their non-Jewish neighbors. We fear, in our bones, that such stereotypes reinforce latent anti-Jewish sentiments and we wonder out loud what it will do to us.

But is that fair? Must a Jewish character in fiction always be pure and saintly? Are there no mean and grasping Jews? Must public relations take second place to the truth? And could it be that the same movie, or book, which stirs our Jewish sensibilities is seen by our non-Jewish neighbor as only an interesting piece of fiction about our times?

In 1978, the Orthodox movement convened a panel of religious leaders to consider proposed solutions to the "ethical problems confronting the Orthodox Jewish community." Harold M. Jacobs, president of the Union of Orthodox Jewish Congregations (UOJC), commented that "it is time for the Orthodox community to come to grips with the continuing embarrassment and 'chillul hashem' inflicted upon it by a very small number of irresponsible but highly visible individuals. I am confident that in the few cases where ethical abuses are found to exist, it would be possible for us to rectify the situation without damaging headlines or recourse to the civil authorities.

"The experienced religious leaders who will conduct this session will explore the avenues open to the Orthodox community to clean its own house and maintain the high ethical standards which are some of the key distinguishing features of our religious heritage."

Why did the Orthodox leaders do this? Did the scandal of the person convicted for defrauding the government in his Jewish old age homes contribute to this concern? Were the leaders right to deal with this? What could they do about it?

In short, are we Jews over-sensitive? Could it be that the literature of some so-called "Jewish" writers and others hold up aspects of our Jewishness from which we recoil because they contain elements of truth, preferring instead our own self-admiring public relations image? Or, is the picture of the Jew which emerges from such writers caused by their own self-hatred and unresolved childish hang-ups in regard to their own Jewishness? We were much more comfortable when our image was one of society's victim, symbol of humanity, and champion of social justice. We do not like to see ourselves presented as successful acquisitors, part of the American Establishment, purveyors of vulgar bar and bat mitzvah celebrations and conspicuous weddings, suburban fat cats, and rapacious business people. But all this is also a part of our deepening assimilation to contemporary American reality and it is questionable to attribute such portrayals automatically to anti-Semitism.

ARE WE JEWS SECURE IN AMERICA

Today, for the first time since the end of World War II, American Jews are seriously worried about the extent and danger of anti-Semitism in America. Only a few short years ago, the American Jewish community regarded itself as both secure and mature; we boasted that anti-Semitism was at a low, virtually insignificant level. But today some Jews in America feel embattled. Some feel we Jews are "up against the wall." For the first time in years, the question of domestic anti-Semitism has risen to an important place on the agenda of Jewish organizations. The generation gap is at work here, too, as the older generation of Jewish people is deeply and emotionally exercised about this danger, while Jewish youngsters tend to think their parents are building mountains out of anti-Semitic molehills. Is this because most Jewish youngsters have never experienced anti-Semitism?

What has happened in the last few years? Part of the answer lies outside America. We are only one generation removed from the Holocaust. Jews who lived through that nightmare are emotionally seared for the rest of their lives. When the Arab powers in 1973 proclaimed their intention to liquidate the State of Israel and drive every Israeli into the sea, Jewish consciousness was heavy with unendurable pain and fear. Similarly, when the Arabs announced their intention of committing genocide against two million Jews in Israel, Jews everywhere looked to the conscience of the world—the United Nations, the leaders of Christianity, the nations of the world—to speak up strongly, to condemn such savagery, and to say to the Arabs and the entire world, "*No More Auschwitz!*" But the world seemed, once again, to have a different agenda, and the fate of Jews did not seem to rank high. Indeed, the United Nations itself became a party to the vicious anti-Semitic lie that Zionism is racism!

This cold sense of isolation which Jews felt once again was not completely abated by Israel's victories. Indeed, the world seemed to be better prepared psychologically to mourn and bless a martyred and defeated Israel, as the world did the six million Jewish victims of the Holocaust, than to face up to a militarily triumphant Israel even if it were victorious in a just cause. So Jewish nerves continued raw, particularly as the passage of time saw Israel falsely painted more and more as an uncompromising, tough, militaristic state while the Arabs began to emerge in the propaganda battle as the poor, pitiful victims of alleged aggression.

Jewish nerve-ends were jangled also by the ugly campaign of anti-Israel and anti-Jewish propaganda which began to pour out of the Soviet Union after the Six Day War. The Soviets broke relations with Israel. In their vile propaganda, they compared Israel to the Nazi aggressors. The venomous nature of this campaign cast a new and dark shadow over three million Jews still sealed inside the Soviet Union. It caused anxiety in Israel, for hadn't the Russians recently brutalized Czechoslovakia, matching their words to their deeds? In neighboring communist Poland, Jews were subjected not only to anti-Jewish propaganda but were harassed and hounded out of many professions and government jobs. The Polish terror campaign demonstrated once again that anti-Semitism has a mad momentum of its own, that anti-Semitism can go forward even in the absence of Jews. Poland's once great Jewish population of three million had been virtually erased by the Nazis. Now, only 16,000 Jews remained. But this did not deter the communist leaders from blaming the Jews of Poland for the student unrest, the economic troubles of the entire nation, as well as for dual loyalties (because of Jewish sympathy for Israel). These events also affected the psyches of American Jews.

American Jewish reactions to anti-Semitism in America must be understood against this backdrop of ominous anti-Jewish developments in many parts of the world. But events within America also heightened Jewish fears. The Arab oil embargo in 1973 made Jews feel desperately vulnerable and alone. Economic recession created widespread joblessness and despair. The decline of many large cities in America sharpened tensions and conflicts and turned our urban centers into social dynamite with mounting violent crime and disabling fear in the streets. The impact of affirmative action programs for minorities—a program which in its application often took the form of quotas and reverse discrimination—touched raw Jewish nerves. The emergence of KKK and Nazi groups in Skokie and several other cities has deepened the sense of Jewish anxiety. In 1980, a pro-Nazi candidate for attorney general in North Carolina got over 40 per cent of the vote; an avowed KKK supporter won a primary contest for Congress in California. How could this happen?

Another disturbing new factor of anti-Semitism in America is the emergence of blatant and vocal anti-Semitism on the part of some Blacks. The phrase, "Black anti-Semitism," has become commonplace. It has also become a red flag for Jews. But how serious is Black anti-Semitism? Studies by the Anti-Defamation League and other groups demonstrate that anti-Semitism is not greater among Blacks than it is among white Christians in America. Many of the old and new points of friction between the two groups were discussed in Chapter 1, "Race Relations," and the ultimate story remains to be written.

The Jewish community has every right to condemn all anti-Semitism, whether Christian, white, or Black. We know that anti-Semitic words, throughout our history, have often led to pogroms and even worse. But it is also important for Jews not to lose perspective.

We can find no safety in turning inward upon ourselves, severing our links with the general community. We can find safety only if we help America to deal not only with symptoms —hatred, rage, bigotry—but with the root problems of our society—slums, powerlessness, decay of our cities, and unemployment—which spawn the evils of bigotry and conflict.

Jews cannot be safe unless America makes it as a nation. Our task as Jews must go beyond the defensive job of countering the attacks of anti-Semites of whatever stripe. Our task remains to bring to the world a vision of a just and peaceful order for all.

9

RELIGIOUS LIBERTY, PUBLIC EDUCATION

A LIVELY CONVERSATION

"Do me a favor," Shane Ferges-
sen was shouting. "Don't talk to me about principle! Principle is
what has got the Jewish community into such a pickle! If I hear
one more speech from you community relations fellows about
standing up for principle, I'll retch!"

Fergessen is a remarkable and paradoxical Jewish type. A
bona fide intellectual, he has contempt for his fellow intellectuals who are alienated from Jewish life; a sharp critic of the
Jewish establishment, he is as knowledgeable about Jewish
life as any Jew in town. Mostly, he is a professional devil's
advocate, a gadfly, at the Friday evening Oneg Shabbat.

"Please, Shane, don't get yourself so excited," I soothed.
"You'll have apoplexy. Besides, the rabbi is looking at us
nervously again, as if we're going to start another pogrom.
Now, quietly, what is it that has you so worked up about
principle?"

152

"Don't talk to me about the rabbi, either," he exploded. "He's another principle-spouter and if he . . ."

"Shush, Shane," I broke in, "you're foaming at the mouth. Start from alef, please. Exactly what are you talking about? Give me one for instance, please."

"I'll give you five, not one," he roared, sloshing the coffee over the rim of the paper cup and taking a fierce bite of the sponge cake. Two eager congregants, hopeful of combat, edged over to listen.

"One, Shane, I'll settle for one," I said.

"Okay. Separation of church and state. Big principle, right? Build a high wall of separation. No aid to religion, right? So you and your friends went to court to defend the rights of atheists. You challenged every little Christmas carol in the public schools. You declared war on Bible reading. And where did it get you?"

"Where?" I echoed. "It got us tremendous victories in the Supreme Court, striking down religious practices, Bible reading, and the Lord's Prayer in the public schools. It got us . . ."

Shane waved me aside. "Bopkes," he exclaimed. "Those things are big fat nothings. You won the skirmishes, but you lost the war. You think the Regents Prayer is going to loom in history? You should live so long. The only real issue in the whole church-state grab bag is federal aid to parochial schools. Cash on the barrel-head. Gelt! Did you win that with all your magnificent walls and principles?"

"Come off it, Shane. You know the Jewish community is divided on aid to parochial schools. The Orthodox want it; most others oppose it as a matter of constitutional principle."

"Precisely," Shane retorted. "That's it precisely! It was a scandal. It was a scandal to elevate a position into a principle. What's the principle? Absolute separation of church and state? Borsht! I don't see Mt. Sinai Hospital refusing federal funds. So we scream absolute principle and end up painting ourselves into an absurd corner—isolated and cut off from the mainstream of American thought!"

"Okay, wise guy," I countered. "If not principle, what then *should* dictate our positions?"

"Circumstances, events, cases, needs, priorities, common sense—I don't know. But to proclaim the purity of Principle —with a capital *P*—is to put our feet into cement, to be a foolish voice in the wilderness. So now you have your principle and the nation has an education program. The real situation was that we had to have a massive federal aid program, that it couldn't be done without token help to church schools and that that price was not too high to pay to save our system of public education. That must be clear even to you!"

"What is clear to me is that we now have made the parochial schools partners with the public schools and that, in the not too distant future, we will have a mushrooming of church schools and a serious weakening of our public school system."

"Oh, spare me the old chestnut about the camel's nose in the tent and all the figures about Holland or wherever it is. What you and your friends call principle is not principle anyway. It's basically fear of the Catholics. And also a foolish pretension that a clear line can be drawn between church and state. And what is the proud result of standing for your principle? You've been hanged from the gibbet, you've been hoisted and shackled, you've been . . ."

"Shane, my boy," I interceded, "we lost a battle, but so long as we don't sacrifice our principle, we will yet win the war."

"War?" he roared. "War? That brings me to my second example. The battle to give tuition credits to parents whose children go to private or parochial schools or to college. You opposed it, repeating your old weary battle-cry of 'separation of church and state.' You should have understood the mood of the people and, since you can't lick 'em, join 'em. There's a middle class revolt out there, my friend. They're sick of shelling out taxes for the poor. They want something back for themselves. And they're right!"

"Shane, Shane," I cried. "Tax credits for parochial schools will kill the public schools, it will finance segregationist private schools, and it will wreck the First Amendment. Even *you* know that!"

"What I know is *reality*. Reality is the public schools are dying anyway, white people are leaving in droves. And reality number 2: Our Jewish day schools are springing up like mushrooms. Jewish kids there are getting a real Jewish education. So why should we be stuck on the old one-note slogans? Let's get a piece of the action and go along to get along instead of being automatic nay-sayers for dead causes!"

"If I understand you right, Fergessen," I broke in, "you're a gutless character. You would have us say amen to everything. You're afraid to have Jews dissent. You're afraid to see the Jewish community stand up and say No! I say when Jews take the popular position, we're in trouble. You'd have us sell out for expediency every time the wind changes. You're a chameleon, Fergessen!"

Fergessen was now latched on to my lapels. "I think I am getting to you, that's why you are calling me names. It is very simple. I have no faith in absolute and eternal principles. I believe in life, in reality, in flexibility, in change, wisdom. Absolute principles are millstones around the neck. In this age, a group, a people, a nation which cannot change cannot survive. Change is the law of life. Can't you see that or are you too blinded by our little rulebook of set principles to see what is happening all around you?"

"Expediency," I shouted, "that's what you're preaching. If we listen to you, we'll go around with our fingers up to the wind. We'll count noses before we take a position. We'll sell out to the highest bidder. We'll speak only when spoken to. We'll run out on the very principles and ideals which Judaism gave to the world and for which Jews stand today."

What was happening all around me was that half the congregation had pressed in to enjoy the vicarious pleasure of a bloody, non-violent debate. I groped for the most effective verbal haymaker I could swing (on the way home I thought of a better one, of course). "Listen, do you think we Jews could have survived all these centuries if we had lived according to your ideas?"

Fergessen surveyed his circle of listeners, looked at me pityingly and murmured softly: "Nu, bubbele, and how else do you think we survived?"

At this point, our wives appeared, as they always do when Shane and I square off at the Oneg Shabbat, to shut off debate.

RELIGIOUS LIBERTY

Here again—a real dilemma. The members of the Jewish community have been America's strongest champions of separation of church and state. Have we been too strict, too absolute in our defense of the First Amendment? And, in any event, does that stand now run counter to our own interests in supporting all-day Jewish schools, the maintenance of which may well require some measure of public funding? Have we, as Shane argues, painted ourselves into a corner? If some public schools are failing to maintain the quality of education which Jews cherish, should we not reexamine our old commitments and reassess our stand? Or is the firm separation still the best for us Jews because it is best for America?

There are many students of American Jewish life who believe that the Jewish commitment to separation of church and state is one of the greatest contributions which Jews have rendered to the enlargement of American freedom. Bear in mind that the US is the first country in the history of the world to build its society on the foundation of separation between church and state; many scholars feel this is America's finest contribution to civilization and the chief guarantee of religious liberty. The First Amendment is the cornerstone of American freedom. It says: "Congress shall make no law respecting an establishment of religion or prohibiting the free exercise thereof."

Particularly in the twentieth century, when Jews had become strong and secure enough to play an active role as a community, Jewish groups have fought to eliminate religious practices in the public schools and to prevent federal aid to parochial schools. They have taken this position not because of any biblical mandate; indeed, ancient Israel was a theocratic state and modern Israel has not yet achieved a full measure of religious liberty. Nor have Jews been moved by opposition to the idea of parochial schools or by prejudice against other religious groups. They have been moved by their own long historical experience which demonstrated that, whenever the state was controlled by the church, Jews—and freedom —suffered. Only in America have Jews been free to pursue their faith, equal under law and practice, and to organize their communal lives. Jews also have learned, through history, that both religion and the state flourish best when they are separate. Thus, America—and its Constitution—created a system of religious liberty which has proved to be both fair and effective. Jews have felt a deep stake in the preservation of this system and in the maintenance of the strictest possible separation between church and state.

The Jewish community has been especially zealous in combating in the public schools such religious practices as Bible reading, the recitation of the Lord's Prayer, the celebration of religious holidays, releasing children from public school to attend religious training in religious institutions. Frequently, Jewish organizations went to court to challenge practices which seemed to contradict the First Amendment to the Constitution. Indeed, Jewish organizations played a crucial role in supporting the McCollum Case in 1947, in which an atheist challenged the released time program (in which children were released for an hour of religious instruction) in Champaign, Illinois, public schools as an infringement of the Constitution. The Supreme Court upheld McCollum and declared released time on public school premises unconstitutional. Later, Jewish groups joined in legal challenges against such practices as Bible reading and the Lord's Prayer in the public schools, arguing that religion belongs in the church, the synagogue, and the home, and not in the public school where every child, including the non-believer, is entitled to be free of any religious compulsion or coercion, however subtle. The Supreme Court has sustained these challenges, and these practices are now, for the most part, slowly being eliminated from the public schools. The essential doctrine of the Supreme Court has been stated as follows:

"The establishment of religion clause of the First Amendment means at least this: neither a state nor the federal government can set up a church. Neither can pass laws which aid one religion, aid all religions, or prefers one religion over another. Neither can force nor influence a person to go to or to remain away from church against his will or force him to profess a belief or disbelief in any religion. No person can be punished for entertaining or professing religious beliefs or disbeliefs, for church attendance or non-attendance. No tax in any amount, large or small, can be levied to support any religious activities or institutions, whatever they may be called, or whatever form they may adopt to teach or practice religion. Neither a state nor the federal government can, openly or secretly, participate in the affairs of any religious organizations or groups and vice versa. In the words of Jefferson, the clause against establishment of religion by law was intended to erect a wall of separation between church and state."

These decisions by the Supreme Court have not been universally popular with the American public. Propaganda campaigns by right-wing and fundamentalist groups have sought to depict these decisions as antireligious and as "eliminating God from the public schools." Some senators and congressmen each year have tried to put through Congress a constitutional amendment which would override the Supreme Court and permit religious practices, such as prayer, in the public schools. Thus far, despite noisy and emotional campaigns, the sponsors of such amendments have failed. The good sense of the American people has recognized that tampering with the Bill of Rights is not a wise procedure. Most Americans realize that the courts have not attacked God or religion but have, as a matter of fact, preserved the integrity of religion by preventing the development of a lowest-common-denominator "American public school religion." By struggling for church-state separation—and speaking out against the intrusion of any religion, including Judaism, into the public school—Jewish groups have faced deep controversy. But they have been faithful to what they regard as fundamental to American democracy.

FEDERAL AID TO EDUCATION

The struggle against federal aid to religion has not been quite as successful. This is—and always has been—the most fundamental issue in the sphere of church-state relations. Until recently, the United States had never given massive public funds to private and parochial schools. Indeed, the long-standing conflict among religious groups—with most Jewish groups siding with most Protestants against federal aid to sectarian institutions, Roman Catholic groups favoring it—was the rock against which such legislation foundered.

But the legislative impasse was broken in 1965 with passage by the United States Congress of the Elementary and Secondary Education Act. For the first time, large-scale federal aid to education was made available. The legislation was made possible by increased awareness that the American public school was in desperate straits and could only be rescued by massive federal funds; by the felt need to strengthen our educational establishment to compete more effectively with the Russians in the cold war; by a shift away from absolute opposition to church-state compromise on the part of Protestant groups; and by the insistence of then President Johnson that a broad education program must be the cornerstone of the "Great Society" which he sought to create in American life. The 1965 Education Act was born out of great hopes. It was also born out of a compromise on the church-state issue, the consequences of which will not be fully clear for many years.

It is difficult to determine the extent to which American

traditions of strict separation of church and state have been affected. But it is known that considerable federal funds have flowed into parochial elementary and secondary schools of all faiths. It is known, for example, that a disproportionate amount of the funds expended under Title 1 of the act (Title 1 provides funds for "compensatory education" for millions of school children whose background of poverty offers them little hope for successful schooling) has been expended on parochial schools. Although only 6 percent of all children participating in Title 1 programs in 1968 were from private and parochial schools, more than 20 percent of the regular school-day projects, involving non-public school children, were conducted on church or church-school premises. Funds have been used to support programs within parochial school classrooms that were not contemplated by the law. Funds are being allocated for programs to serve children enrolled in parochial schools without proper regard to the relative number of such children who come from economically deprived backgrounds. In some communities, a fixed percentage of funds is allocated to non-public schools without prior determination of the numbers of children coming from poverty backgrounds. While these may or may not be violations of the act, and of church-state separation, it has thus far not been possible to bring these practices to the Supreme Court for a judgment as to their constitutionality.

Why are some Jewish groups so strongly concerned about federal aid to non-public schools? Because they believe that such aid undermines the separation of church and state. Also, Jewish agencies are committed to the preservation of the public school as perhaps the most important training ground for democratic values in our society. The experience of many nations has been that public aid to non-public schools results in a weakening of public education, the growth of a separate network of parochial schools, and a deepening conflict among religious groups to secure public funds. In the Netherlands, for example, state aid to church schools has resulted in a situation in which public education has declined and 80 percent of the children go to various church schools. In addition, this situation often leads to religious-based political parties, competing for public funds. Most Jewish agencies feel that such a development in America would be a disaster for religious liberty and for American democracy. Because private schools can select among applicants while public schools are open to all, there is fear that publicly aided private schools would become the schools of the white middle class while public schools would become "pauper schools," primarily serving poor nonwhites. At bottom, of course, is a question of justice: Does the government have a right to take my tax money and give it to a church whose religious teachings are not mine and which may, indeed, violate my deepest religious conscience?

The Jewish community, in recent years, has split on the key issue of federal aid to parochial schools. The Orthodox community, which itself maintains a large and growing system of day schools, believes that federal aid to religious schools is not a violation of separation of church and state. Like the Roman Catholic community, which maintains a costly separate school system, Orthodox Jewish groups have argued that America must take responsibility for the education of every American child, no matter what kind of school he or she may go to. Most Jewish groups continue to believe that, while a person has every right to send a child to a non-public school, he or she has no right to ask the government to pay for it. The public school, in which every child has an equal place as an American, deserves every bit of assistance which the American taxpayer makes available. This issue continues to be the central issue in church-state relations. It has now become a key and controversial issue within Jewish life itself.

The main argument advanced by persons advocating public aid to non-public schools is that certain benefits of a welfare nature, such as medical and dental examinations and hot lunches, should be provided to children in all schools, private as well as public. Such benefits are widely provided, and they rarely evoke any objection, since they clearly benefit the individual child and not the school. But advocates of federal aid to parochial school extend the "child benefit" theory to benefits of an educational nature, too, on the premise that they, too, aid the child rather than the school. Opponents of federal aid to parochial schools argue that the "child benefit" theory must not be stretched into an indirect means of channeling public funds to parochial schools. It is feared that the "child benefit" theory may eventually be used to justify the building of parochial schools and the payment of salaries to teachers in church schools. For, after all, isn't that also ultimately for the benefit of the child?

In every argument on separation of church and state, it is always pointed out, correctly, that the US has never had complete and absolute separation of church and state. We have chaplains in the armed forces; presidential Thanksgiving proclamations; "In God We Trust" on our coins; tax exemptions for churches and synagogues; and many other examples of government aid to religion. Some of these practices are *not* violations of church-state separation. Others are not significant. Still others do lie in the twilight zone between constitutional propriety and impropriety. But, despite these and other such practices, the validity of separation of church and state is well established in American life. It continues to require the vigilant and vigorous support of all who regard the First Amendment as our best guarantee that religious liberty will continue to flourish in the US and that "relations between a man and his Maker are a private concern, into which other men have no right to intrude."

The US Supreme Court, in 1973, reaffirmed its position that federal aid to parochial schools is unconstitutional.

A QUESTION OF PRIORITIES

Two decades ago, the maintenance of separation of church and state was one of the highest priorities of the American Jewish community. Jews, together with a few like-minded groups, led the public efforts to keep religious teaching, ceremonies, and practices out of the public schools. They helped to secure milestone Supreme Court decisions that religion belongs in the church, the synagogue, the home rather than in the public domain. In these efforts, the Jewish community spoke with one voice as a united community. While many Americans felt strongly that "God must not be banished from the public schools," history will record that Jewish action did much to safeguard religious liberty for all Americans, believers and non-believers, Christians and Jews.

But there has been a change in America and in the Jewish community. Church-state issues no longer command the attention of the media or the public. Within the Jewish community, church and state is no longer a priority issue; indeed, the nagging problem of church-state separation *in Israel* seems to be of more compelling concern to American Jewry than are the remaining church-state problems here. In fact, this is a mark of success. Many of the old issues have been disposed of by legal action; i.e., distribution of Gideon Bibles, Lord's Prayer, Bible reading, etc. Moreover, on the new issues—tuition credits for parochial schools, voucher plans, etc.—the Jewish community is now deeply split, thus neutralizing Jewish influence and impact. The Orthodox community stands with the Roman Catholic community and segments of Protestantism on the key issue of public monies for parochial schools.

Did the Jewish community make too much of a fuss about "the wall of separation"? There are those in the Jewish leadership who think so. They say we were too absolute, properly objecting to the intrusion of sectarian practices but unwisely combatting also innocuous-seeming programs to "teach *about* religion and religious values." They say we risked serious and emotional community and interfaith conflicts in many cities and suburbs by challenging insignificant Christian practices such as Christmas carols, silent prayer, and others. They say we eroded our position as a faith group by lining up with atheist and secular groups in court tests and public controversy. Perhaps we did occasionally overreact, but in the main Jews as a group served as a definite force for religious freedom and American pluralism.

THE SURVIVAL OF PUBLIC EDUCATION

But the real crux of evolving Jewish opinion about the importance of church-state separation is the changing Jewish attitude toward public schools. Charles Silberman, in his *Crisis in the Classroom,* described the growing sense of disappointment and dissatisfaction with public education. He described the "pervasive sense of crisis" brought about by the many charges of failure against public schools. Most schools, he said, not only fail to educate children adequately but are "grim," "joyless," and "oppressive" places. The sharpest indictment of the public school is for its failures in educating Blacks and other poor children. Some critics contend that the schools have also failed middle-class children, many of whom are not equipped to read and write even after graduation from high school.

Inevitably, Jews share in this malaise. Indeed, the Jewish lust for education makes Jews even more sensitive to any shortcoming in public education. As the historic Jewish honeymoon with the public schools began to fade, Jews, like others, examined alternative educational systems, including private Jewish day schools.

Is this a betrayal of public education? Do we lessen the chance to correct the failures of public education when we put our own children in private schools? Are we copping out? Perhaps to some extent, yes, but are we obliged to send our children to schools which we feel are inadequate merely because they are *public?*

And what is the magic and virtue of *public* vs. *private?* In the past, we Jews saw public education as the fundamental transmitter of democratic values—the place where children learned to live with persons of diverse faiths and backgrounds —the place where American pluralism came alive—the place which equipped our Jewish immigrants and their children to live in a new, vibrant, and free American culture.

Do we still? To some extent, yes. Despite all the negative rhetoric about public schools, there are many superb school systems throughout America, especially in wealthy suburbs which lavish large sums on the public schools which are the proud ornaments of the community. Because most Jews are suburban, middle-class, and education-motivated, we tend to live in precisely these communities. The heavy choices do not fall on those living in Great Neck, or Beverly Hills, or Shaker Heights, or Scarsdale, but upon those in New York City, Los Angeles, Cleveland, Detroit, and every other metropolitan center.

For most Jews living within the large cities of America, faith in the viability and efficacy of public education has been shattered. Integration has seemed to become a futile chess-game, with children used as pawns, arousing violent tumult without improving the quality of education. Besides, most large cities no longer have enough white kids for integration. Logic says involve the metropolitan areas, including the suburbs, and make integration meaningful; but logic is no match for overwhelming political opposition. So, despite everything, few schools really give students a living experience in diversity across racial, religious, and economic lines. Most would be satisfied if their students could read at grade level. Then what is the special holiness of the public school?

How serious is the condition of public education? Is it beyond repair? The decline of academic standards seems quite steep. Since 1963, national average scores on Standard Achievement Tests (SAT) have fallen 49 points in verbal aptitude and 32 points in mathematical aptitude. Clearly our public schools turn out too many young people who are functional illiterates. And if secondary and high school education are graduating young people ill-equipped in the fundamentals of reading and writing, it is not surprising that, according to the Carnegie Foundation for the Advancement of Teaching, the deterioration is felt at the college level. Each year 40 percent to 60 percent of the students at the University of California find themselves required to enroll in remedial English.

A report by the Carnegie Foundation concluded that "general education is now a disaster area, which instead of being shaped by a coherent educational philosophy is often determined by a number of internal and external forces—faculty interests, student concerns with the job market, 'relevance,' social fads, and the like."

Vital as minority programs are for the total society, it is unavoidable that such programs have further weakened academic excellence. At some schools, the average SAT scores of the disadvantaged students are nearly 200 points lower than those of other students. The national average for minorities is 100 points lower than that for non-minority students. In New York City, high school graduates are now reading at the eighth grade level—a shocking decline in one decade. The decline is accompanied by mounting violence, vandalism, disruption, and disorder, further impairing the climate of education.

This deterioration of mass education is leading to mass stupidity—a fatal environment for democracy. Illiterates are not likely to know or care about their rights. Some 47 percent of a sample of seventeen-year-olds did not know the elementary fact that every state elects two senators. One out of two of these youngsters believed that the president appoints members of Congress. What does this mean for the great dream of universal public education which was to cultivate a community of informed and civilized citizens as the very bedrock of democracy? How can democracy survive the intellectual wasteland of a television age and a "Me Decade"? Can public education be rescued from swift decline? How? Jews—along with all other concerned persons—must deal carefully with such questions.

This disillusionment has inspired a flowering of Jewish day schools. They are booming within Conservative Judaism, and the Reform Movement—which had once bitterly opposed day schools as a threat to public education—now has a few day schools in the US and Canada—and more in the offing. The passionate opposition has melted away. A strong determination to give our children an excellent Jewish education —something beyond the brief hours which a Sunday school education affords—predisposed many Jews to consider the alternative of the Jewish day school. That positive impulse, plus the negative response to the problematic aspects of the public schools, has brought a large and continuing change to the Jewish community of America.

What will America's future look like if these trends accelerate and the public schools become widely separated from the elite private and day schools for those with the means to escape? Will this put America on the road to apartheid—a separate and unequal society? What will be lost if the public school collapses? And if that something is significant, how can we stop saying premature kaddish and do something to pump new life into the patient while there is still time?

10

PROPOSITION #13, TAX REVOLT, ECONOMIC JUSTICE

What's a Jarvis? Until 1978, Howard Jarvis was regarded as an elderly, harmless, right-wing odd ball who couldn't get elected dog catcher in California. For years he lurked about the edges of state politics as a public scold, complaining about high taxes and public education and other menaces to the Republic. Then, in 1978, he organized the Jarvis Referendum intended to cut California's property tax by a whopping 33 percent at one fell swoop. As in his past efforts, politicians airily dismissed him as a crank and scoffed at his proposal as so outlandish that there was no need to consider the massive damage which passage would mean to the educational and social welfare needs of the people of California. However, as the moment of truth for the referendum approached, it was clear that Jarvis had touched off a tidal wave. His referendum swept California by an overwhelming 2 to 1 vote, burying every public official who had tried to plug the leaking dike.

Jarvis had unleashed a true revolution, not only in California but throughout the nation. He didn't create it. The indignation, the frustration, and the fury were there, boiling under the surface, waiting to erupt. His genius was to recognize these emotions and to give them a political focus. What Jarvis produced in California was an electrifying "message" to politicians in every state and in Washington. What was the message? It was loud and clear: *"Government has become too bloated and wasteful, it is stifling the individual taxpayer, it is reversing the basic truth that the government exists to serve the citizen and not the other way around."* Besides, said Jarvis, throwing massive funds at social problems does not even *work*!

The surging support of Californians stemmed, in part, from inequities and mistakes in California's taxing policies. But, clearly, voters in every state of the Union—burdened by escalating property taxes at a time when they were being strapped by inflation—responded to the clarion call of taxcutting with the zeal of angry rebels whose long-delayed revolution was finally at hand.

Who voted for Proposition 13? It was a political tidal wave, carrying Republicans and Democrats, conservatives and liberals, cutting across virtually every category of race, economic class, religion, and geography. It is, therefore, unfair to attribute passage of Proposition 13 to kooks and right-wing reactionaries. But it is also true that the *effects* of such a drastic approach to taxes must be significant cuts in education, health, service to the elderly, and social welfare. The impact of Proposition #13 was eased by the fortunate fact that the state of California had accumulated a six billion dollar surplus which was used to cushion the shock. But what if that had not existed, as it does not in most other states? And even in California, despite the surplus, it is clear that programs to serve the *poor* had to be trimmed, or eliminated as a result of the drastic Jarvis roll-back.

It is of interest that only two groups in California resisted the onslaught of the Jarvis tax revolt. The first was racial minorities—Blacks and Hispanics—who saw in the revolution an unspoken but strong racist attack on minority groups and especially welfare programs directed at them and their families. The other was Jews who—while divided on Jarvis—cast a slim majority of their votes against the referendum. Why should Jews have voted against their own pocketbook interests? Why should they have voted with poor people and minorities rather than with their peers—middle-class Episcopalians and Methodists—in the economic system?

The same questions have often been asked about our Jewish political behavior. Why were Jews the only white ethnic group to have given a majority of its votes to Jimmy Carter in 1976, joining with America's Blacks rather than with other white ethnic and religious groups in our political choices? No other white group of voters has displayed a similar propensity to vote against its own immediate pocketbook interests. A recent poll, for example, showed a majority of Jews willing to support guaranteed annual income for all Americans! At a time of growing neo-conservatism, Jews have been reluctant to join the new popular mood of distrust of government, which insists that government cannot solve social problems such as poverty and that it should stop wasting our money trying to do so.

This is a dilemma for Jews. We, too, are burdened by ever-mounting taxes. We, too, are angered by waste and corruption which frequently infect government at the local and national level. The revelation of bribe-taking by congressmen in the Koreagate scandal—in which some US representatives were bought with cash bribes by an arrogant South Korean dictator—horrified us along with all other Americans. The Abscam scandal, showing congressmen ready to take bribes from a mythical wealthy Arab in order to fix legislation, reminds us of how sorry governmental delivery systems can be. So why aren't we Jews foremost on the barricades of the tax revolt? What are we waiting for? What's our dilemma?

There are two equally strong explanations. The first is an enduring conviction that, in the long run, Jewish security is safeguarded by a decent and compassionate society which seeks actively to help the disadvantaged, the poor, the handicapped, the elderly, and all other unfortunate persons.

Only in such a stable and tranquil society can Jews be safe. Jews can never be secure in a tormented or unjust society which can explode in rage and division. And if government doesn't care about the weak, who will? This is the explanation of Jewish liberal traditions and the Jewish belief that government must use its resources to diminish suffering and misery for those who need a governmental hand the most. Our definition of enlightened Jewish self-interest has helped to shape our social and political attitudes in democratic America.

But it is not only contemporary self-interest. There is a second explanation, and it goes to the heart of our religious and historic heritage. It is that our Jewish ethical system compels us to be concerned with the unfortunate and the stranger in our midst. An American observer, commenting on America's recent War on Poverty during the Great Society, observed that the first anti-poverty program in human history was spelled out in the Hebrew Bible. The first true welfare society was fashioned by our ancestors. Our self-interest is reinforced by profound ethical impulses drawn from a Jewish religious value system which commands us to be co-partners with God in building a just and peaceful world. For a detailed analysis of Jewish teachings on poverty, see appendix at end of this chapter.

But is the dilemma real? If we Jews want to stick with our liberal, big-government, free-spending convictions, what's the dilemma? The dilemma is that we are human, like everybody else. We live in a Me Decade, where the public mood is not much interested in spending money for "them," where personal fulfillment is much more attractive than bold social programs. We live in a time of political disillusionment with the efficacy of government itself. We live in an America where the pressures of inflation make it difficult, if not impossible, to contemplate extensive social innovations, such as national health insurance. And we are told that even the massive spending involved in the War on Poverty did not wipe out poverty or even significantly dent it. Our noble campaign of racial integration has resulted in re-segregation, the collapse of public education, and angry divisions among our people, without benefiting our racial minorities. The litany goes on. The disenchantment with both government and liberalism is becoming a primary feature of our political landscape, and the drum-beat of the tax revolt is heard in every state and in the federal government as well.

Are Jews immune from such prevailing moods? We are not. Has the time come to reconsider our traditional liberalism? Could the convictions of yesteryear be out of tune and harmful to dealing with the new realities? More and more American Jews think so. Are they right? The Jewish dilemma—on this as on many other burning issues—is real and painful and important indeed!

FAREWELL TO JEWISH LIBERALISM?

For Jews, the new mood in America had a particular bite. Jews, beyond any other ethnic or religious group, had adopted the liberalism which emanated from the New Deal and which was renewed by a succession of Democratic successors to Roosevelt. Clearly that Jewish identification with Democratic liberalism was coming into question. The Jewish vote continued to be largely Democratic, but with smaller and smaller margins in every election. Major Jewish voices (such as the magazine *Commentary*) exhorted Jews to abandon "knee-jerk liberalism" which, they said, had run out of intellectual fuel. They challenged Jews to vote their real "interests" instead of their obsolete traditions and habits. "Is it good or bad for Jews?" became the new slogan of hard-nosed pragmatism, implying that instinctive Jewish support for "liberal" programs—public housing, racial integration, church-state separation, affirmative action, civil liberties, welfare, etc.—was now against *real* Jewish interests. These arguments shook and challenged a troubled Jewish community. The organized Jewish community moved perceptibly to the right. Neo-conservative intellectuals dominated the debate on Jewish public policy. Jewish liberals, like liberals everywhere in America, went on the defensive.

Having abandoned the ideas of the New Deal, what new ideas did liberalism offer to meet the emerging challenges? The center of gravity of Jewish political opinion seemed to move from Scarsdale to Queens. It seemed only a matter of time before Jewish liberalism would disappear and Jews would become like everyone else.

But, as always, Jewish behavior defies all predictions. Immediately after the elections of 1978, a survey of Jewish voting behavior was conducted by CBS and *The New York Times*. The survey concluded that, despite their widespread disapproval of President Carter, American Jews remain "far more liberal" than any group of voters. Noting that Jews vote more heavily than other groups (2.7 percent of the population; 4 percent of the voters), the survey found that 72 percent of the Jews polled voted for Democrats for Congress in 1978 in contrast to Roman Catholics (60 percent) and Protestants (45 percent). Of the Jews polled, 36 percent called themselves "liberals," two times higher than other religious groups, and only 16 percent called themselves "conservative." The survey found voting Jews most strongly in favor of abortion rights (including government aid to poor women), civil rights for gay people (including the right of teachers in public schools, 59 percent to 33 percent). Jews overwhelmingly supported cuts in the defense budget, arms agreements with the Soviets, and they were less interested than Americans generally in a constitutional amendment requiring a balanced budget. Strikingly, more than half of those interviewed reported that they had household incomes of $25,000, a watershed level at which other respondents to most questions had become more conservative. As in the past, Jewish political attitudes contradict their own pocketbook interests. Obituaries for the death of Jewish liberalism are—at the very least—premature.

Where does this stubborn strain of Jewish liberalism stem from? This too has been heavily analyzed. Is it a mindless, unexamined persistence in political attitudes appropriate to an earlier age? Is it a response to a widespread historic intuition that Jews are safer on the left side of the center than on the right? Is it a recognition that Jewish enlightened self-interest is best served in a liberal, harmonious, active society and that liberalism can best insure such conditions? Is it a product of the Jewish ethical and religious heritage which, in the freedom of American pluralism, is free to express itself more freely than at any other time in Jewish history in the Diaspora? Is it merely a time-lag?

Students of Jewish political behavior find several of these factors interacting, but few deny the impact of Jewish ethical traditions and values. Activist, this-worldly, intellectual, stressing deed over creed, affirming the Jew's prophetic obligation to serve with God in building a just and humane world—these Jewish qualities appear to have retained their vitality and influence on the mind and behavior of today's Jews. Even as we Jews become secularized, shifting increasingly from our religious moorings, we seem unable to escape the moral weight of prophetic teachings along with centuries of Jewish stress on justice, mercy, compassion, peace, and mitzvot.

JUDAISM AND POVERTY

(Excerpt from *There Shall Be No Poor,* by Richard G. Hirsch, former director of the Religious Action Center, Union of American Hebrew Congregations.)

"When you have eaten your fill and have built fine houses to live in, and your herds and flocks have multiplied, and your silver and gold have increased, and everything you own has prospered, beware lest your heart grow haughty and you forget the Lord your God, who freed you from the land of Egypt, the house of bondage . . . and you say to yourselves, 'My own power and the might of my hand have won this wealth for me.' Remember that it is the Lord your God who gives you power to get wealth. . . ." (Deuteronomy 8:12–18)

Judaism rejects the concept of "survival of the fittest." We are not engaged in a struggle for survival against our fellow human beings. Our sages say, rather, "Not only does man sustain man, but all nature does so. The stars and the planets, and even the angels sustain each other."

Human life is sacred, so sacred that each person is considered as important as the entire universe. Biblical ethics are permeated with laws assuring protection of the poor. The Bible prescribes that when a field is harvested, the corners are to be left uncut; the field is not to be gone over to pick up the produce which has been overlooked. The gleanings of orchard and vineyard are to be left untouched. All that remains is for the poor, the stranger, the orphan, and the widow.

Every seventh year was a sabbatical year, during which the land was to lie fallow, and that which grew of itself belonged to all, "that the poor of thy people may eat." (Exodus 23:11) All debts were to be cancelled. Every fiftieth year was a jubilee year, during which all lands were to be returned to the families to whom they were originally allocated. The law of the fiftieth year was too complex to be observed and fell into disuse in Jewish history, but the spirit behind the law was preserved. Our ancestors realized that an unrestricted pursuit of individual economic interest would result in massive concentrations of wealth for the few, and oppressive poverty for the many. They sanctioned competition, but they rejected "rugged individualism." The intent of the law was to restore the balance, to give those who had fallen an opportunity to lift themselves up again. Land was not the permanent possession of any human being. "The land shall not be sold in perpetuity; for the land is Mine; for ye are strangers and settlers with Me." (Leviticus 25:23)

Jewish ethics sanction the institution of private property. However, Jewish tradition never asserted that property rights take precedence over human rights—an assertion made by many in America today. Nor did Judaism accept the Puritan emphasis on the acquisition of property and worldly goods as a sign of virtue. On the contrary, for the Jew, human rights have priority over property rights. The tithe prescribed in biblical law was not a voluntary contribution, but an obligation imposed on all, in order that "the stranger and the fatherless and the widow shall come and shall eat and be satisfied." (Deuteronomy 14:29) Any person who was hungry could help himself or herself to the produce in a field at any time, without asking permission of the owner, so long as it was not carried away to be sold for profit.

No person had absolute control over personal property. Those who cut down young trees in a garden were to be punished for wasting that which did not belong to them. The person who owned a well in a field had to make the water available to the inhabitants of a nearby community. Such requirements evolved out of the fundamental Jewish conviction that material possessions are gifts from God, to be used for the benefit of all people.

The poor person, as much the child of God as the rich person, has been disinherited from his or her Father's wealth. Unlike some religions, Judaism does not encourage the ascetic life. Poverty is not the way to piety. Scarcity does not lead to sanctity. The search for holiness is not made easier by insufficiency of basic necessities.

The common saying "Poverty is no disgrace" may offer consolation—to those who are well off. As a statement of morality, it would have much to commend it—"Poverty *should* be no disgrace." As a statement of fact, however, it is totally inaccurate. Poverty *is* a disgrace—for those who are poor. Poverty is destructive to the human personality. "The ruin of the poor is their poverty." (Proverbs 10:15)

Our sages taught that poverty was the worst catastrophe that could happen to a person. "If all afflictions in the world were assembled on the side of the scale and poverty on the other, poverty would outweigh them all." The afflictions of poverty are so severe that Jewish tradition makes the seemingly radical statement that "the poor man is considered as a dead man." Poverty is spiritual death. Judaism has never drawn a distinction between body and soul as other religions and systems of thought have done. The Jew knows that a person's values are in great measure shaped by life experiences. "Where there is no sustenance, there is no learning," declared a teacher of the first century. To feed the mind, the body must also be fed. A chasidic rabbi of the nineteenth century expressed it well when he said, "Take care of your own soul and of another man's body, not of your own body and of another man's soul."

TZEDAKAH

There is no word in the Hebrew vocabulary for "charity" in the modern sense. The word used is tzedakah, which literally means "righteousness." Tzedakah is not an act of condescension from one person to another who is in a lower social and economic status. Tzedakah is the fulfillment of an obligation to a fellow-being with equal status before God.

Injustice to humanity is desecration of God. "Who mocks the poor blasphemes his Maker." (Proverbs 17:5) Refusal to give charity is considered by Jewish tradition to be idolatry.

Our sages taught that Abraham was more righteous than Job. According to rabbinic tradition, when great suffering befell Job, he attempted to justify himself by saying, "Lord of the world, have I not fed the hungry and clothed the naked?" God conceded that Job had done much for the poor, but he had always waited until the poor came to him, whereas Abraham had gone out of his way to search out the poor. He not only brought them into his home and gave them better treatment than that to which they were accustomed, but he set up inns on the highway so that the poor and the wayfarer would have access to food and drink in time of need. True charity is to "run after the poor."

Acts of charity are the means but not the end. The end is to restore the image of the divine to every human being. The sensitivities of recipients are to be safeguarded at all times. "Better no giving at all than the giving that humiliates." "One who gives charity in secret is even greater than Moses." In the Temple at Jerusalem, there was a "chamber of secrecy" where the pious placed their gifts and the poor drew for their needs—all in anonymity. The same practice was observed until modern times. In every synagogue, a charity box with a sign "Matan Beseter" (an anonymous gift) was placed.

The Talmud recounts the lengths to which great scholars went in order to protect the self-respect of the poor. A rabbi and his wife, accustomed to giving alms while recipients were asleep, were surprised when one poor man awoke. In order not to offend him, they jumped into a still heated oven, risking serious burns. Another rabbi would tie money in a scarf and when he was near a poor man, would fling the gift over his back, so that the poor man would not have to suffer the embarrassment of facing his benefactor.

Even greater than tzedakah was "gemilut chasadim," or "acts of lovingkindness." "One who gives a coin to a poor man is rewarded with six blessings, but one who encourages him with kind words is rewarded with *eleven* blessings." Gemilut chasadim was considered superior to almsgiving in three ways: "No gift is needed for it but the giving of oneself; it may be done to the rich as well as to the poor; and it may be done not only to the living but to the dead."

In connection with funeral practices, an early custom had evolved to bring the deceased into the house of mourning in expensive caskets of silver and gold, whereas the poor were placed in wicker baskets made of willow. The Talmud decreed that everyone should be placed in wicker baskets "in order to give honor to the poor." To this day, Jewish tradition frowns on lavish funeral practices.

THE DIGNITY OF THE RECIPIENT

Jewish tradition wrestled with the problem of how to preserve the dignity of recipients of charity. The rabbis based much of their discussion on the commandment, "If there be among you a needy man . . . thou shalt surely open thy hand unto him, and shalt surely lend him *sufficient for his need in that which he wanteth."* (Deuteronomy 15:7, 8) The phrase "that which he wanteth" was interpreted to mean that if a man did not have sufficient funds to marry the community should assume responsibility for providing him with the means to support a wife. The phrase "sufficient for his need" became the peg on which to hang the concept that a man was entitled to be sustained at a standard of living to which he had become accustomed. One Babylonian rabbi sent his son to give a contribution to a poor man on the eve of Yom Kippur. The boy returned to his father and complained that the poor man was not in need since the boy had seen him imbibing precious old wine. Over the protest of his son, the rabbi doubled his normal contribution, on the grounds that the gentleman had been used to a better life than the rabbi had originally thought. The Talmud recounts how the great scholar Hillel, learning of a man of high station who had become poor, gave the man a horse to ride, and when he could not find a servant to run before him, as was the man's custom, Hillel himself ran before him for three miles.

The verse from Deuteronomy quoted above also became the basis for a highly developed system of loans. Throughout rabbinic literature, a loan is emphasized as the finest form of charity. "Greater is he who lends than he who gives, and greater still is he who lends, and with the loan, helps the poor man to help himself." Almost a millennium after this was written, the medieval philosopher Maimonides defined the various types of charity and categorized them into his famous "eight degrees of charity," the highest of which is to enable a person to become self-supporting. Until modern times, every Jewish community had a "gemilut chesed" society, whose primary purpose was to grant loans to the needy without interest or security.

Our tradition recognized that an outright gift, no matter how well-intentioned, still might instill feelings of inferiority in the receiver. However, a loan is a transaction between equals. Sometimes the loan was a delicate fiction. In those instances, where a poor person is too proud to accept a gift, one should offer a loan, even though one might never expect to have the money returned, and then subsequently the loan could be considered as a gift.

The rabbis dealt in a direct fashion with those who in our day would be called "freeloaders," the poor who exploit the system of welfare. They looked askance at beggars who went from door to door. A person should exert every effort not to be dependent on others. "Skin the carcass of a dead beast in the market place, receive thy wages, and do not say, 'I am a great man, and it is beneath my dignity to do such work.'" Nevertheless, even though the rabbis maintained a severely critical attitude toward imposters, they were generally liberal in offering them assistance. They realized that even those who made false claims served some purpose. "Be good to imposters. Without them our stinginess would lack its chief excuse."

JEWISH WELFARE

In the talmudic period, the Jewish community supplemented the obligations of private charity with an elaborate system of public welfare—the first in history. Jewish tradition has always been nurtured in and through the community. Hillel's famous "Do not separate thyself from the community" sets the pattern. Even Jewish worship is a communal experience. Almost all prayers, including those recited by an individual in private, are written in the plural. So it was only natural for the Jew to look upon poverty as the responsibility of the entire community. The existence of the poor was an indication of social inequity which had to be rectified by society itself. The system of social welfare became the means of restoring integrity to the community.

The practices and theories of Jewish philanthropy anticipated many of the most advanced concepts of modern social work and became the basis for the excellent programs and high standards of American Jewish welfare agencies. The organization of Jewish welfare evolved through the centuries, but the principles were established during the second century.

Every Jewish community had two basic funds. The first was called "kuppah," or "box," and served the local poor only. The indigent were given funds to supply their needs for an entire week. The second fund was called "tamchui," or "bowl," and consisted of a daily distribution of food to both itinerants and residents. The administrators of the funds were selected from among the leaders of the community and were expected to be persons of the highest integrity. The kuppah was administered by three trustees who acted as a bet din, or "court," to determine the merit of applicants and the amounts to be given. The fund was operated under the strictest regulations. Collections were never made by one person, but always by two, in order to avoid suspicion. The collectors were authorized to tax all members of the community according to their capacity to pay, and, if necessary, to seize property until the assessed amount was forthcoming. All members of the community were expected to contribute, even those who were themselves recipients of charity—testimony to the principle that no individual was free of responsibility for the welfare of all.

By the Middle Ages, community responsibility encompassed every aspect of life. The Jewish community regulated market prices so that the poor could purchase food and other basic commodities at cost. Wayfarers were issued tickets, good for meals and lodging at homes of members of the community who took turns in offering hospitality. Both these practices anticipated "meal-tickets" and modern foodstamp plans. Jewish communities even established "rent control," directing that the poor be given housing at rates they could afford. In Lithuania, local trade barriers were relaxed for poor refugees. When poor young immigrants came from other places, the community would support them until they completed their education or learned a trade.

The organization of charity became so specialized that numerous societies were established in order to keep pace with all the needs. Each of the following functions was assumed by a different society in behalf of the community at large: visiting the sick, burying the dead, furnishing dowries to poor girls, providing clothing, ransoming captives, supplying maternity needs, and providing special foods and ritual objects for holidays. A host of other miscellaneous societies were formed to cover every possible area of need. In addition, there were public inns for travellers, homes for the aged, orphanages, and free medical care. As early as the eleventh century, a "hekdesh" or "hospital" was established by the Jewish community of Cologne—primarily for the poor.

In a sense, American Jews provide "proof positive" that properly conducted community welfare programs are not deleterious for individuals or for a society. In part, at least, American Jews are products of the welfare-oriented civlization of Judaism. Yet, contrary to the admonitions of opponents of welfare programs, Jews have not developed the characteristics of dependency which are supposedly in store for such persons.

11

CRIME AND PUNISHMENT

In 1978, a poll was taken in New York City to measure public attitudes on the issue of capital punishment. The poll was taken at a time when support for the death penalty had reached a high level of intensity, so it was no great surprise that 68 percent of the respondents expressed the wish that the death penalty be re-instituted in New York State. What was more surprising was that among *Jewish voters* the demand for the death penalty was even higher (69 percent)! *New York Jews,* traditionally regarded as particularly liberal and humanitarian, voting in favor of capital punishment! What was going on?

What was going on was another emergent dilemma—a collision of values between traditional Jewish liberalism and the surging demand for tougher measures to crack down on the violence which is epidemic in America and to achieve some measure of law and order on the streets of our cities and safety in our homes.

But Jews *for capital punishment,* that relic of barbarism which most rabbis and Jewish organizations have condemned for decades? How could that be? Simple. Some of our cities have become virtual jungles. More murders are committed each day in America than in the rest of the world combined.

Muggings are committed in many of our cities in midday, on streets filled with passers-by. Subways and schools have to be patrolled with an army of police. Shoplifting is so common that the merchants merely raise their prices and write the shoplifting into overhead. Elderly people have become special prey to human predators—many never leave their apartments anymore. Fear keeps people at home, especially at night, behind double-locked doors, prisoners in their own homes. The media numbs us with daily horror stories of violence run amok. And rarely is the culprit apprehended. And, if apprehended, seems often to get a slap on the wrist and is back on the streets for further action in short order.

It is no wonder there is a sense of outrage. Jews share in that outrage. Moreover, many of the victims are elderly Jews, trapped in the old neighborhood by poverty or illness or habit. Violent assaults on human beings is the crime which most frightens Jews. Even if anti-Semitism is not involved, the fact of a gang of youthful thugs beating a Jewish merchant or an elderly woman on the street evokes a frightening spectre of pogrom in the Jewish mind. That the criminals are often Black or Hispanic reinforces racial bigotry and fear; it is no help to point out that minority persons are also the chief *victims* of violent crime.

It is not "illiberal" to demand an end to such savagery. We have no stomach for the long view that the criminal is the product of society's failures and that reconstructing society is the surest way to reduce crime. Nobody is prepared to wait for the long range. Life and property are in jeopardy now. Daily life has become too anxiety-provoking. The jungle does not make for personal tranquility, nor does it engender calm thinking about the nature of the problem and a reasoned search for solutions.

So we are all vulnerable to manipulation. Our hunger for quick solutions is often so strong that we seek simplistic and facile answers. Shrewd politicians seize on our fears, and they exploit our anxieties. Re-institution of the death penalty has become the vote-getting buzz-word response of many politicians to the public cry for law and order.

For Jews this raises an ironic paradox: the religious justification for the death penalty is based on the Hebrew scriptures but the evolution of Jewish law came to abhor the death penalty and Jewish persons and organizations have led the fight for abolition.

That Judaism developed as a religious way of life expressing itself in law is well known. It is not nearly so well known, however, that Jewish law underwent thoroughgoing changes over the centuries, both within the biblical period and thereafter. It developed in accordance with the specific requirements of each era and place, and the legal principles through which the Jew could fulfill an eternal covenant with God. But this creative legal evolution took place within the traditional Jewish belief that the totality of law, unto all eternity, was given to Moses at Mt. Sinai.

Early Hebrew society was primitive and so were its laws. Capital punishment was frequent for crimes considered trivial by later generations. But those later generations could not easily repeal the ancient law. It was divine in origin; it was eternal. They could and did, however, arrange that literal enforcement of the law became impossible. For example, the law with regard to punishment for assault is quite clear: "Eye for eye, tooth for tooth, hand for hand, foot for foot, burning for burning, wound for wound, stripe for stripe." (Exodus 21:24) Yet we know that, early in the evolution of Jewish law, money fines were substituted for these corporal punishments and the law as written was never enforced. According to Deuteronomy (21:18–20) a "stubborn and rebellious son" could be turned over to the elders of the city who could order him stoned to death. The law was clear, but it was not carried out. In all of rabbinic literature, there is not one case cited of a rebellious son being executed. That law, like all laws pertaining to capital punishment, apparently remained purely theoretical and was not applied in practice.

DEATH PENALTY

For the death penalty prescribed in Deuteronomy, the restrictions in Mishnah Sanhedrin 8 are so numerous that the effect has been virtually to abrogate the death penalty. In Mishnah Makkot 1:10, a court is branded as "murderous" if it imposes the death penalty as often as once in seven years; according to Rabbi Eleazar ben Azariah, once in 70 years. Rabbi Tarphon and Rabbi Akiba opposed the death penalty altogether 1,900 years ago!

There is ample evidence in the Talmud and in other Jewish legal literature through the centuries that these sages were not alone in their stand. It was impossible for the rabbis to abrogate capital punishment altogether; God had ordained it in His word. But they certainly did their best to make it impossible of accomplishment!

Only deliberate murder was punishable by death. Previous hatred, treacherous lying in wait, the use of a deadly weapon had to be proved. The murderer had to know the nature of the act and the severity of punishment—before he or she committed it. And, most important, *two* witnesses were necessary to establish the commission of the murder.

Legal restrictions like these made Judaism's concept of justice deeply humanitarian. Increasingly, punishment for a variety of crimes was transferred from the jurisdiction of any court to that of God alone. Rabbinic authority always remembered that Judaism is not a harsh legalistic system but the living faith of "merciful children of merciful parents."

In our day, liberal Jews have not hesitated to continue the Jewish process of testing ageless principles in the light of contemporary knowledge. Many Jews have been in the vanguard of the movement against capital punishment, for prison reform, and to bring up to date and liberalize our concepts of justice.

Nothing in Christian or Jewish teachings is contrary to the idea that churches and synagogues deal with contemporary problems of crime, punishment, and juvenile delinquency.

Indeed, the basic values of Judaism and Christianity require serious grappling with these problems which have grown to a major moral crisis in American life. As campaigns mount to restore the death penalty, we must recall that, in its origin, capital punishment was conceived as revenge. Modern advocates of this practice stress it as a deterrent to other murderers and capital offenders. This contention was already challenged in 1923 by Dr. George W. Hirchwey, a renowned penologist:

"On June 21, 1877, ten men were hanged in Pennsylvania for murderous conspiracy. The *New York Herald* predicted the wholesome effect of the terrible lesson. 'We may be certain,' it said, editorially, 'that the pitiless severity of the law will deter the most wicked from anything like the imitation of these crimes.' Yet, the night after this large scale execution, two of the witnesses at the trial of these men had been murdered and, within two weeks, five of the prosecutors had met the same fate."

Capital punishment by hanging was practiced in England up to the eighteenth century and often became a public spectacle. There was no evidence that the crime rate lessened. As a matter of fact, pocket-picking became so prevalent in the audiences gathered to watch the public hangings of pickpockets, it was eventually decided not to have them in public any longer.

There seems little, if any, correlation between the severity of the punishment and the frequency of crime. Minnesota and Michigan were just as safe as Iowa and Illinois even when the former two states had outlawed capital punishment.

In addition, the possibility of judicial error cannot be overlooked. Our system of justice is fallible because human beings are fallible. In 1955, in New York, Louis Hoffner, who had been convicted of murder and had already served twelve years of a life sentence, was pardoned on the basis of new evidence which had become available. Such grievous errors occur. But what if Hoffner had been given death instead of life imprisonment?

Capital punishment is an inhumane anachronism. It is

frequently argued that gas and electrocution have made death painless, but even this has been seriously questioned. Aside from physical pain, the mental torture preceding such a "painless death" is beyond calculation. In addition, the torment and stigma inflicted upon relatives, who have committed no crime, are savagely cruel. Perhaps worst of all is what it does to society itself. Capital punishment not only seems futile in deterring crime; it is also a brutalization of the human spirit and an arrogation of the lifetaking power which inheres only in God.

Until 1979 when Florida executed John Spenkelink, capital punishment seemed to be fading out of American life. No person was executed in the United States between 1967 and 1973; every state awaited the Supreme Court's decision on the constitutionality of the death penalty. Finally, in 1972, the Supreme Court spoke, but it did not end the debate. The court said that the unequal *application* of the death penalty, which is usually reserved for the poor and minority group members, *did* represent "cruel and unusual punishment" and was unconstitutional. It left open the question if the death penalty itself is unconstitutional. Today, as advocates of capital punishment push the death penalty as an answer to mounting crime, many states are drawing up laws which would pass the Supreme Court's strictures. There is still no evidence that the death penalty is a deterrent. But the debate continues in every state and community until such time as the Supreme Court makes its ultimate decision in this matter.

GUN CONTROL

The proliferation of guns in the hands of Americans, abetted by easy access and availability, is considered a major cause in the horrendous crime rate afflicting our country. Then why is nothing being done to control the ownership of guns, beyond a few measures which in the light of reality are totally ineffective?

Rabbi Jerome K. Davidson, religious leader of Temple Beth-El of Great Neck, New York, is one of the many Americans who puzzled over this question and got angry about the answer. Although a heavy majority of Americans supports gun control, few care enough to speak out and try to mobilize public action. Rabbi Davidson not only spoke up from his pulpit; he sent his views to *The New York Times*, which published his letter (entitled "Trophies of Ineffective Gun Controls") on February 13, 1979.

"To the Editor:

"Brenda Spencer, a San Diego sixteen-year-old, last week momentarily diverted our attention from the big news made by strife in Iran and visitors from China. She did it by opening fire with a .22-caliber rifle on an elementary school, killing two and wounding nine, including children ranging in age from 7 to 12. 'I don't like Mondays. This livens up the day. I just started shooting for the fun of it.'

"Of course, we reacted with outrage and utter revulsion. I am certain most of us were genuinely depressed by the grisly occurrence. But then what? Even now, the memory begins to fade.

"Needless to say, the incident reflects a multitude of problems. Drugs may have played a role. The question of parental supervision seems almost too absurd to raise. The mounting mood of violence in the world obviously wields its deadly influences, even in the cities of sunny California. These are very difficult issues, and they seem out of reach for those who would strive to prevent such disasters in the future.

"Or is that a cop-out? There is no excuse whatsoever for a .22-caliber rifle, with 500 rounds of ammunition, to have fallen into that girl's hands. She didn't steal it. It isn't a trophy someone brought home from the war. She received it for Christmas! Someone gave it to her as a present.

"Such tragic occurrences are not rare. Who does not recall the college student who gunned down 45 people, killing 14, from the top of a tower at the University of Texas? Have we already forgotten the mass killing in New Rochelle less than two years ago by an American Nazi whose apartment contained an entire arsenal? Have we pushed the ugly memory of the Son of Sam killings out of our minds? I cannot erase from my thinking the funeral years ago of the teenager in our community who was killed when he and a friend were toying with a gun someone had brought to his home.

"These shattering events reflect the unwillingness of Americans to admit to the real danger that the private possession of guns represents to our very lives. There are 40 million handguns alone in the United States, one is sold every 13 seconds. Twenty-five thousand people are shot to death each year, 69 each day. But it is evidently not enough to cause the American people to overpower the National Rifle Association and demand the enactment of effective controls.

"It has already been said, 'With all the violence and the murders and the killings we have in the United States . . . we must keep firearms from people who have no business with guns.' Yet we do not heed the words, despite the dramatic fact that they were spoken by Robert F. Kennedy five days before his assassination.

"What happened in southern California can happen on the north shore of Long Island. Will a greater tragedy be required before the American people are moved to act? Until we do, our children's lives will depend on whether or not someone decides to open fire on them just for the fun of it."

A few weeks later, the gun lobby, which the rabbi attacked, took careful aim at him, using paid advertisements in several Long Island newspapers to publish on May 10, 1979, the following open letter to the residents of Great Neck and all Nassau County communities, signed by another rabbi.

"The exhortation of Rabbi Jerome K. Davidson (of Great Neck), in his letter to *The New York Times* (published on February 13, 1979), that the American people should 'overpower the National Rifle Association and demand the enactment of effective (gun) controls,' makes less sense than an exhortation that the American people should overpower the

American Civil Liberties Union and demand the repeal of the exclusionary rule which prevents the use in court of illegally seized evidence.

"After all, every day many vicious criminals and murderers go free merely because the police blundered in the search and seizure of the evidence which must therefore be excluded at the trial on account of the exclusionary rule; yet, the Civil Liberties Union and the courts properly contend and insist that the Fourth Amendment of the federal Bill of Rights in the Constitution, 'the right of the people to be secure in their persons, houses, papers, and effects, against unreasonable searches and seizures,' protects the illegally searched criminal. So why shouldn't the Second Amendment in that same Bill of Rights, 'the right of the people to keep and bear arms,' protect the law-abiding citizen? And, in an excess of zeal, should we muzzle the First Amendment rights of the freedom of speech and advocacy of the National Rifle Association?

"The solution to the problem of violent crime cannot possibly be found in any panacea like gun control (prohibition) legislation, any more than you can change lead into gold merely with a philosopher's stone, or any more than you can cure alcoholism with Prohibition legislation. And let us not forget that alcohol alone kills more people every year in this country than firearms.

"Firearms have often been the only hope of oppressed and persecuted peoples. With but ten pistols, the Jews in the Warsaw Ghetto chased out the mechanized Nazi German war machine and forced the German army into house-by-house combat and the burning down of that ghetto in order to conquer it. Later in Budapest in 1944, the Nazis realized that they could not then afford a repetition of the Warsaw uprising. For that reason they waited in their extermination of the Jewish community of Hungary until they were able to enlist the cooperation of the Hungarian Jewish leadership. This the Nazis were unfortunately able to do, to reassure the Jews and persuade them to go quietly to their extermination by keeping the horrible destination a secret. The Nazis perceived that armed resistance by even a handful of pistol-toting Jews in Budapest would necessitate house-to-house combat with troops they could not then afford.

"Historically, Jews and other minorities have much to fear from gun control laws—laws which have been selectively enforced, inevitably against ethnic, religious, and political minorities all over the world. Therefore, any additional legislation on this subject must be approached with great reservations."

So the issue was joined. Which rabbi is most in accord with Jewish values? Would the possession of guns by Jews in Germany really have prevented the Holocaust from taking place? Is gun control good or bad for Jews? The background paper, prepared by the Commission on Social Action of the Union of American Hebrew Congregations (UAHC) setting forth its stand on firearms legislation, will help you to clarify this issue.

FIREARMS CONTROL LEGISLATION

By Marc Saperstein, professor of Jewish Studies at Harvard University.

Every two minutes a gun is used to kill or wound an American citizen. More than 7,500 Americans were murdered with firearms during one year. Since 1900, three-quarters of a million people have died in the United States by guns—through murder, suicide, and accident. This is 200,000 more than the number of Americans killed in all of our wars.

These statistics of the Justice Department confirm the impression made by the tragic assassinations of the last two decades that our country has, in the words of the President, "a record of violent death and destruction that shames our history."

Most Americans, knowing that there is no civilized nation in which it is as easy for mental incompetents, drug addicts, criminals, and minors to purchase firearms as our own, have long wanted to take action to change this. A Gallup poll in 1967 showed that 85 percent of all adult Americans were in favor of firearms control legislation, including the registration of all guns. This high percentage has remained fairly constant during the last thirty years. Yet the wishes of the majority for a sensible control of firearm sales have been stymied by the powerful lobbying led by the National Rifle Association and various gun manufacturers.

What are the arguments of the opponents of firearms control legislation?

1. They maintain that the right "to keep and bear arms," guaranteed in the Second Amendment to the Constitution, would be violated by such legislation.

2. They are afraid that gun control laws would hurt the responsible sportsman who uses guns for hunting and marksmanship.

3. They claim that the legislation would not lower crime rates, as criminals would still be able to obtain firearms illegally.

These arguments are unfounded.

1. The Second Amendment states: "A well-regulated militia being necessary to the security of a free state, the right of the people to keep and bear arms shall not be infringed." This obviously was written in order to guarantee each state a militia, and the Supreme Court has stated many times, in upholding the constitutionality of gun control laws, that it does not apply to individual citizens bearing arms. In 1939, the Court held *(US vs. Miller)* that "the Second Amendment applies only to those arms that have a reasonable relationship to the preservation of efficiency of a well-regulated militia." Furthermore, the courts have established that rights given by the Constitution are not absolute and have recognized the government's power to limit such rights in the interests of the general welfare and domestic tranquility. The right to bear arms must be subordinated to the

right to life. There may be a constitutional right to own an automobile, but the automobile must still be registered and anyone who wants to drive it must be licensed.

2. Sensible gun control legislation would not interfere with the legitimate use of guns by the responsible hunter or marksman in any way. In nations with strict firearms laws, hunting still thrives. During the two years since the enactment of the law controlling the purchase of guns in New Jersey, the sale of hunting licenses increased. Legislative measures which would help eliminate the irresponsible firearms owners and set standards of competence for firearms usage should indeed increase the prestige, and certainly the safety, of gun sports. The purpose of gun control legislation is not to prevent legitimate ownership of firearms, but to keep such arms from those who would misuse them.

3. No one claims that gun control legislation is the solution for violence and crimes. But the fact is that it does cut down both the incidence of crimes in which guns are involved and the general rate of violent crimes. In states with strong firearms laws, the percentage of homicides in which guns are used ranges from 30 to 40 percent; in states with weak laws, the range is from 60 to 70 percent, and the rate of murder is two to three times higher than in the former group. A comparison of our country with other nations is even more revealing. In countries which require registration and licensing, the rate of gun murders is 5 to 50 times lower than ours: 2.7 per 100,000 population in the United States, as against .52 in Canada, .12 in West Germany, and .05 in Britain.

Estimates of the number of firearms owned by private citizens in the United States range from 50 to 200 million. Each day the papers carry stories of personal tragedy caused by someone who should not have been allowed to own a gun. Each year brings new national horror at political assassinations which threaten the foundations of the American system of government. The situation deteriorates, the rate of gun crimes increases as a small minority blocks the remedy.

The results should affront the conscience of all. To delay action further would be unpardonable.

THE PRISON SYSTEM

Beyond the issue of guns is the broader issue of crime and punishment in American life. If a prison system is the barometer of a society's moral values, America has little reason for pride.

The stark truth is that we have not yet cast off the medieval concept that society's responsibility toward criminals is to punish them. We have talked much of the need not only to isolate criminals to protect society but also to rehabilitate them if possible. Some improvements in this direction have been made in our prison systems, but essentially they still represent, more than anything, institutions of social vengeance. Incarcerated for years in a fortress-like, forbidding institution, surrounded by a high massive wall; subjected to the deadly, demoralizing routine of prison regimen; placed in contact with hardened criminals and sex perverts; deprived of normal sexual and affectional needs—this is not the way to reclaim the lawbreaker. It is the way to stifle hope, to break the spirit, to warp already disturbed personalities, to deepen hostility and aggression against society, to prepare a person for a life dedicated to crime.

Students of American criminology have long been aware that our prison system is a demonstrated failure. The American prison system was developed one hundred and seventy years ago through the leadership of the Quakers (Society of Friends) who conceived it as a humane alternative to widespread corporal and capital punishment. Over the years, American prisons have improved in some respects, but it is doubtful that even the modern prison is really much better than the system of corporal punishment. Five or ten years of gradual rotting behind prison walls are at least as demoralizing as fifty lashes.

Prison routine is more cruel than any form of corporal punishment. But, unpleasant as it is, does not the modern prison accomplish its purpose? Apparently not. If the purpose is to deter the criminal from committing another crime, statistics prove that our prisons are failing badly. In one Massachusetts state prison, 70 percent of the inmates had previously been in prison. In the Eastern Penitentiary of Pennsylvania, 67 percent of the prisoners had been in prison before. In New York, as many as 80 percent of the men sent to prison had previous prison experience. More than half the convicts in all our prisons have previously been convicted of one or more crimes. If punishment prevented crime, there might be some justification for our present prison system. But it doesn't. On the contrary, we could not devise a system better calculated to transform troubled youngsters into confirmed, chronic criminals. In his book, *The Psychology of the Criminal Act and Punishment,* the distinguished psychiatrist Gregory Zilboorg summarized the views of most students of this subject:

"We must bear in mind also that punishment, despite the traditional belief to the contrary, has apparently no deterrent effects on crime. Since punishment does not precede but follows the antisocial act and, in addition, does not seem to exercise any deterrent effect on crime, it would be a gross error indeed to consider the traditional penal system as a system of social defense."

But it may be asked, Don't our prisons try to rehabilitate the prisoners? On paper, yes. Penologists have repudiated, as incompatible with our scientific insights, the idea that the prison exists for punishment. They speak of the need for curative treatment and rehabilitation, psychiatric and psychological attention for every prisoner. Rare is the American prison which actually has a program of this kind. Some progress has been made in some federal prisons and the more enlightened system developed in California under the leadership of former Governor Earl Warren. On the whole, however, our prisons are still primarily instruments of punishment. Why?

Some students of criminology contend that this is what the

public wants, that the American public accepts the premise that persons who have transgressed against society must be punished. If this were not the premise of our thinking, they argue, we would have, long ago, demanded that our present prison system be completely overhauled. Harry E. Barnes and Negley K. Teeters, in their authoritative *New Horizons in Criminology,* attribute our failure to dislodge the present prison system to a "convict bogey," an exaggereated fear of men who have been convicted of a crime. They insist that we want the criminal punished because we project onto him the burden of our own sins and by punishing him we expiate our sense of guilt. This attitude results in what they call a "jail psychosis" in the American people which makes impossible a realistic appraisal of our prison system and necessary citizen action to bring the system into line with logic, modern scientific knowledge, and the religious principles of compassion and mercy.

There seems to be a public insistence that prisons punish and not "coddle" prisoners and this attitude tends to dissuade even the most progressive wardens and prison officials from putting modern theories of penology fully into practice. A genuine rehabilitation program requires flexibility and experimentation, but inevitably it also increases the risk of escape. The public will not stand for escapes, and the result is that even the best systems are constantly afraid of public criticism of their daring. If religious groups are indeed the conscience of America, they have a vast task to perform in developing public awareness and sensitivity to the imperative need for drastic prison reform.

That the public has these attitudes toward criminals and their treatment should not be surprising. Freudian theories aside, the root of the problem seems to be that citizens generally are woefully ignorant of the purpose, the methods, the effectiveness, and the ethical implications of our penal system. Far from gaining knowledge of these matters, we are confused and misinformed by the press, television, and motion pictures which, for the most part, prefer to shock and titillate us with lurid crime stories than to inform and enlighten us to the facts of our penal system. Public officials also make little effort to get such knowledge across to the community at large. The result of public ignorance is indifference.

Few Americans are aware of what goes on behind prison walls. Corporal punishment is officially frowned upon, but illegal beatings and whippings are still common. Our prisons are old and housing conditions are bad. We do not have a fraction of the psychiatric facilities we need in our prisons; there are only fifty full-time psychiatrists in the entire American prison system. Guards and other prison personnel from cooks to chaplains are so poorly paid that individuals of high caliber can rarely be attracted. Guards are invariably white, middleclass, and middle-aged, totally lacking rapport with the new breed of black prisoner from the inner city. Food is usually inferior and the way of serving it is even worse. Minimum requirements of privacy and of normal human regimen are seldom respected. Sexual disturbances, homosexuality, and sexual warfare are rife and, even worse, inevitable under present prison arrangements.

PRISONS IN TURMOIL

Recently we have witnessed a virtual epidemic of riots in American prisons. A European penologist, after a careful study of the American prison riots, reported that in virtually every case conditions in the prison were intolerable and that the riots were the only effective weapons the prisoners had to remedy their legitimate grievances; the concessions granted the rioters did, in every case, help to rectify the inexcusable failures of the prison. The significance of these riots, however, goes deeper than bad prison conditions and physical equipment. Prison inmates feel that the only way in which they can win the interest of the public in improving the prison situation is by rioting. Unfortunately, experience tends to confirm their judgment. Nonviolent protests and demands by prisoners are ignored. Riots usually result in improvements. While this does not justify the horror and violence of prison riots, it helps us to understand them. And, above all, it places a blazing spotlight on public apathy about the treatment of prisoners.

Attica was the worst prison disaster in American history. Yet Attica, prior to the bloody riot of 1971, was not all that different from other maximum-security prisons in America. Like all other prisons, it was a forgotten institution, neglected by the public. It housed 2,200 inmates on September 9, 1971. Emphasis was on confinement and security. As in most similar institutions, there were noble words about rehabilitation as an objective of detention, but the shortage of trained personnel and the inadequacy of facilities made rehabilitation a sour and hollow promise. Idleness was the main occupation. No serious program of education was available. Correctional officers were white men drawn from rural communities; they could not communicate with the urban minorities who made up the bulk of the inmates. The inmates were deprived of all civil rights, including the right to send and receive letters freely, to have and to express political views, and the right to be protected against arbitrary and summary punishment by state and prison officials. Beyond all individual and specific grievances was the pervasive feeling among the inmates that they were not regarded or treated as *human beings,* that they were denied any sense of human dignity.

The uprising in Attica, according to the investigation which followed, was not planned. It was a spontaneous explosion of a multitude of grievances on the part of men who could not get the attention of the authorities through normal channels. The rebellion of Attica prisoners was, after several days of acute tension, drowned in blood in an assault by state troopers who retook the institution at a cost of 43 men slain, hundreds wounded, and a searing reminder for all the world that our prison system is a stark and deadly failure. In the end, Attica is every prison; and every prison is Attica.

Much of the trouble is that the prison fortress is invisible to us, the public. Even the judges who commit people to these institutions rarely know the inside of the place they are sending them to. Some judges have begun to make personal inspections of the prisons. After one night in the Nevada State Prison, twenty-three judges from all over the United States came out "appalled at the homosexuality," frightened by the prisoners' "soul-shattering bitterness," and shaken by "men raving, screaming, and pounding on the walls." A judge from Kansas, E. Newton Vickers, summarized his reactions: "I felt like an animal in a cage. Ten years in there must be like 100 or maybe 200." The judge appealed to the state of Nevada to "send two bulldozers out there and tear the damn thing to the ground."

What can be done to improve our penal system? Not minor tinkering but a major overhaul is indicated. It is true that we need new and progressive institutions with more humane concepts of treatment. But there is something more fundamental. One authority contends that our prisons are overcrowded in large part because almost half the inmates should not be in prison at all. Dr. Garrett Heyns, warden of Michigan State Reformatory at Iona and a leading penologist, has stated that one-third of the country's prison inmates ought to be released immediately; these persons were confined for minor infractions and, says Dr. Heyns, do not belong in prison. Many penologists believe that an even higher percentage of our prison population does not belong in prison and that many of the rest should not be subjected to such long sentences. But, if not prison, what?

One answer lies in a greatly expanded use of the modern practice of probation. Probation does not mean that a person committing a crime is absolved of his crime and sent home scot free. It is a method of supervising, assisting, and treating offenders as individuals in an effort to restore them to normal and productive living. Under the guidance of a trained probation officer, the individual can be helped and treated where prison can only incarcerate. Probation—in which a person convicted of an offense is released on suspended sentence under the direction of a probation officer—and parole—in which a prison inmate is released before the end of his sentence on the authority of a parole board—emphasize the rebuilding of the individual rather than public vindictiveness. The expense of community treatment in probation is one-tenth the cost of institutionalization. But, far more important, it reflects a faith in individuals and in our ability to redeem them. It costs us more in many ways to merely cast them into prison and forget them.

No religious group which takes its values seriously should rest content until the American people demand and get a system which will correct and not merely punish, rehabilitate and not debilitate, which will treat prisoners and not merely stigmatize them, which will regard them as human beings whom we must strive to restore to usefulness and not as open targets for societal vengeance. Religious groups in Belgium, England, France, and Sweden are active in campaigns for prison reform which are based on newer concepts and which hope to achieve the "spiritualization of public policy toward the criminal."

Religion has a responsibility in the field of crime prevention, but this responsibility must go far beyond recitation of the well-worn clichés about religion as a magical cure-all. There is in fact little scientific evidence that religion has played a major role in crime prevention. A host of studies show that the proportion of religious affiliation may even be higher among convicts than among the public at large. Religion's role must become a dynamic and positive one in this area.

Obviously, the problem of crime prevention is a highly complex one and is closely interrelated with other major problem areas ranging from the status of the family to economic security, among others. It must be a conscious factor in the consideration of all of these problems. But, in addition, religious people, dedicated as Jews are to a belief in the rule of law in the world, must make the achievement of good laws, respect for them, and obedience to these by all citizens, a primary goal in social action.

REHABILITATION—CAN IT WORK?

Can prisons rehabilitate? On the present evidence, the answer would have to be NO. Could prisons rehabilitate? If the public really cared what went on, if psychological and vocational and educational services were greatly augmented, if new and humane facilities for small prison populations were built, if we could throw off our lust for *punishment*. . . . If, if, if. . . . But are there realistic alternatives to a prison system?

Many bold suggestions have been made. If one is guilty of a crime against property, let one make "restitution" instead of being sentenced to what President Nixon once called a "university for crime." If one is guilty of an offense but is *not* deemed dangerous or unreformable, let him or her be shifted to "community-based corrections," keeping the person as close as possible to family, job, and normal life, instead of being stuck in a cage. Crime commissions have estimated that only 15 or 20 percent of present prison inmates are dangerous or unreformable; the rest should be treated outside of walls and bars. In Sweden, for example, 80 percent of its convicted offenders get a suspended sentence or probation; the Swedish repeater rate is only 15 percent!

Another daring proposal is to do something about the startling fact that 52 percent of all people in jails have *not yet* been convicted of any crime. Of these, four out of five are eligible for bail but cannot raise the cash. Because courts are overcrowded, such unconvicted defendants can rot in cells for months or even years, waiting for a trial. The Vera Foundation in New York City has urged the cancellation of money bail for offenders who can demonstrate job stability or family ties; if this would work, it would cut the US jail population (and expense) by half.

VICTIMLESS CRIME

Another way to cut down crime is to clear the courts of the endless stream of "victimless crimes." While serious crimes of violence and robbery are increasing, half of all arrests are for crimes without direct victims, crimes which bring no calls to the stationhouse switchboard. Each year our police are kept busy arresting four million miscellaneous drunks, loiterers, addicts, prostitutes, gamblers, and vagrants. The reason for this is America's Puritan tradition which seeks to use the law not only to safeguard persons and property but also to protect people from their own sins and vices—even if they injure nobody but themselves.

As America learned during Prohibition, it is impossible to regulate many forms of behavior by law. Today there are many distinguished voices arguing that the only way to save our criminal justice system from its present overclogging, our policemen from wasting their time and energy with lesser matters, and our society from hypocrisy is by getting the victimless crime off the criminal agenda. Let programs of combined medical-social work teams deal with problems that are essentially societal, not legal, and free the police and the courts to deal with dangerous crime which haunts our streets and threatens our safety.

Whatever we do, it will take public awareness and action. Ignorance and bigotry often help to defeat any possibility of rehabilitation now. For example, it is painfully difficult for even a skilled person, who was once in jail, to get a job. Cruel laws deprive the ex-convict of many rights and job opportunities. A classic case is that of Mel Rivers, ex-convict, who was taught to be a barber in prison but could not get a license to practice when he was released. He got a job as a real estate salesman, but he could not get a license for that job either. He tried nursing, but the nursing school refused him because of his record. He sought a job as a security guard in a hospital, but that was denied because the hospital had a policy against ex-offenders. He tried to get bonded as a manager of a movie theater but was turned down. He was even turned down by New York City as a bus driver, even though his employment tests were exceptionally good.

Mel Rivers came within a hair of going back to crime. Is that surprising? Why should one knock one's head against a stone wall in a society that hates ex-convicts? For, even when the law does not deny an ex-convict a chance, the public—employer, manager, personnel director—does. Mel Rivers was saved by the Fortune Society, an organization of ex-convicts which works *for* and *with* convicts and ex-convicts. But he's one in a million.

We need groups like the Fortune Society. We also need an informed and aroused public. Chief Justice of the Supreme Court Warren Burger has said:

"When a sheriff or a marshal takes a man from a courthouse in a prison van and transports him to confinement for a year or two or three, this is *our act*. We have tolled the bell for him. And whether we like it or not, we have made him our collective responsibility. We are free to do something about him; he is not."

12

THE HOLOCAUST

Even the Holocaust—the darkest period of human history—presents dilemmas for Jews. For one thing, there is the question of what lessons to draw from this event, because certainly this cataclysm must have the profoundest significance. But which lessons? To some Jews, the lesson is blunt and despairing: we Jews have to look out for ourselves, because the world does not care whether Jews live or die. Humankind was silent then, it is silent now, and we would be foolish to expect conscience to speak for us in the future. "Never Again" is the slogan of those holding this view—never again will we let them do it to Jews!

There is another—and different—view. It is that the meaning of the Holocaust is never again for any segment of God's family! This view is that the lesson of the Holocaust is that silence is the greatest sin and that sin applies also to Jews if we stand idly by the bloodshed—and holocausts—of other peoples. Therefore, Jews must be involved in the endless task of building a better world.

Remembering the Holocaust is a moral duty for every Jew. But how we remember it, and what that memory impells us to do, will determine the shape of our future. That memory can make us *more* human, *more* Jewish, more committed both to *faith* in the Jewish people and to faith in humankind. Even the Holocaust is a dilemma for Jews!

Simon Wiesenthal is the name most familiar to students of the Holocaust. He has been the Nazi hunter par excellence. Through his Jewish Documentation Center in Vienna, he has succeeded in finding and bringing to trial dozens of hidden Nazi criminals, most notably Adolf Eichmann. A few years ago, Wiesenthal wrote a novel entitled *The Sunflower*. The book is a disturbing and soul-searching study of some of the aching moral dilemmas which were posed by the Holocaust. It is an extraordinary work and includes a symposium of the views of 31 prominent thinkers on some of the profound moral complexities posed in Wiesenthal's novel.

The central issue is stated on the book's jacket: "A young Jew is taken from a deathcamp to a makeshift army hospital. He is led to the bedside of a Nazi soldier whose head is completely swathed in bandages. The dying Nazi blindly extends his hand towards the Jew and, in a cracked whisper, begins to speak. The Jew listens silently while the Nazi confesses to having participated in the burning alive of an entire village of Jews. The soldier, terrified of dying with this burden of guilt, begs forgiveness from the Jew. Having listened to the Nazi's story for several hours—torn between horror and compassion for the dying man—the Jew finally walks out of the room without speaking."

Karl, the Nazi soldier, dies, but the conscience of Simon, the Jew, is deeply disturbed because he had failed to respond to the repentant German. Haunted by the confrontation, Simon discusses his dilemma with fellow concentration camp inmates, with a Catholic priest, and—years later—feels compelled to visit the parents of the repentant Nazi soldier.

The terrible question which agitates Simon for years is: "What should *I* have done?" What should Simon have done? What should he have said? Can Simon, or any other Jew, serve as a representative of an aggrieved group and grant forgiveness in behalf of the entire group? To what extent can the German youth, barely out of his teens, and deeply influenced by a dominating and vicious ideology, be held responsible for his actions? Could Simon find a way to respond to Karl's remorse and need for repentance without going so far as granting forgiveness? One of the symposium writers asked whether Simon, by turning his back on Karl's plea for a forgiving word, did not "participate in Karl's sin." What would be a truly Jewish response, bearing in mind the traditional Jewish emphasis on teshuvah (repentance), the central theme of the High Holy Days? In Jewish tradition, no sin can exceed the infinite grasp of divine forgiveness. Should Simon have taken the position that only God could grant the forgiveness which Karl so ardently sought? But what about the traditional ethical demand that the injured person must grant forgiveness to the genuinely repentant sinner?

But, the respondents to the symposium insist, the question revolves about the sincerity of Karl. It turns out that Karl came from a good family; his father had opposed the Nazis. To the dismay of his parents, young Karl had been caught up in the fever of enthusiasm and joined a Nazi youth group. When war broke out, he volunteered for the SS (the Nazi elite guard). Karl did not go along with the cruel behavior of Nazi troops, and he gave food to Jews at an army base. After he had been compelled to participate in the burning of the village, he was so sickened and overpowered by guilt that he could not and would not participate in further aggressive actions, despite the orders of his superiors. While paralyzed with guilt, he was hit by the exploding shell which led finally to his death.

Did Karl's activities differ from those of American soldiers who participated in the My Lai massacre in Vietnam? Wouldn't a contrite and repentant American soldier deserve forgiveness? Should a German be judged by a different standard?

One of the most searching responses in the symposium came from Dr. Milton Konvitz:

"I cannot speak for your victims. I cannot speak for the Jewish people. I cannot speak for God. But I am a man. I am a Jew. I am commanded, in my personal relations, to act with compassion. I have been taught that if I expect the Compassionate One to have compassion on me, I must act with compassion toward others. I can share with you, in this hour of your deep suffering, what I myself have been taught by my teachers: 'Better is one hour of repentance in this world than the whole life of the world to come' (Avot, IV, 17); . . . It is not in my power to render to you the help that could come only from your victims, or from the whole of the people of Israel, or from God. But insofar as you reach out to *me,* and insofar as I can separate myself from my fellow-Jews, for whom I cannot speak, my broken heart pleads for your broken heart. Go in peace."

All of us are confronted with the nagging moral problem of how we Jews should relate to modern Germans. To forgive? Certainly we cannot place blame on Germans who were not even alive at the time of Hitler. Could we forgive Karl? There are a variety of passionate opinions and feelings among us. Can we *forget?* Never!

WHILE SIX MILLION DIED

A Study Guide prepared by Marc Saperstein, professor of Jewish Studies at Harvard University.

1. Thesis of the Book

While Six Million Died, by the late Arthur Morse, deals with the role of the United States government in relation to the Jews of Eastern Europe from 1933 to 1945. What emerges is a carefully documented account of the incredible, cynical apathy of our government, especially the State Department, regarding the sufferings and the eventual extermination of these Jews. Morse shows how the United States constantly hushed up information about Nazi atrocities against Jews, which poured in from the most reliable sources and generally blocked effective action on behalf of the refugees in Eastern Europe until the beginning of 1944, when it was too late to save more than a fraction of the Jewish population.

There were many proposals urged in vain upon our government even after the war had started. These included easing the Allied blockade to enable relief supplies to be brought into Eastern Europe, liberalizing our immigration rules to expedite the flow of refugees, and urging the Latin American countries to do the same. There were demands that Britain revoke its White Paper of 1939 which drastically limited Jewish immigration to Palestine, pleas for the evacuation of refugees from Spain to South Africa to make room for others in Spain, and putting pressure on the International Red Cross to provide the same safeguards for imprisoned Jews as for prisoners of war or interned civilians. There were also attempts to convince the neutral nations to open their borders to Jewish refugees, to bomb the railway lines to Auschwitz and the extermination camps themselves. Direct appeals were to be made to the Axis powers for the release of the Jews, with an Allied guarantee to find temporary havens until the end of the war. No one knows how many lives could have been saved if any of these proposals had been seriously pursued by our government. The heroic and effective efforts of the War Refugee Board, established in 1944, in saving the lives of thousands of Hungarian and Bulgarian Jews, suggests that countless thousands more could have been saved if such an effort had been started a year and a half earlier, when the State Department first received fully documented evidence that Hitler had ordered the extermination of Europe's Jews.

While Six Million Died is more than a history book. It is a chronicle of human callousness in the face of the overwhelming suffering of others. It is a book which arouses, not only anger about the past, but also raises some crucial questions concerning the future, to be faced by Jews, by Americans, by all people of conscience.

2. Indifference of Christian World

"The one really discouraging element is that the Christian world, in this country and in other countries, should to such a very small extent take in the meaning of this current attack upon the principles of civilized society. Until Protestants and Catholics as well as Jews come to see that the things they hold dear, even as the things Jews hold dear, are threatened—not until then will there be an adequate response to enable refugees from central Europe to be cared for." James McDonald, High Commissioner for Refugees, League of Nations, June 15, 1938.

While there were individual Christian leaders who strongly urged that the Jewish refugees in Eastern Europe be helped in any possible way, more characteristic of the churches, all the way up to the Pope, was silence. Many Jews were again incensed at the silence of most of these same Christian bodies before the outbreak of the Six Day War, when Jews were once again threatened with extermination. What are the implications of this for interfaith relations? Can Jews ultimately rely on any ally when they are really in trouble, except for other Jews? If dialogue is useful, what are the things we must explain to the Christians? Should Jews continue to pursue interreligious dialogue?

3. Public Opinion
To what extent does public opinion, expressed through newspapers, petitions, rallies, etc., influence the policy of governments? The evidence in this book indicates that the governments of Great Britain and the United States did at times respond to public feeling. By 1936, Morse writes:

"Neither the President nor his cautious State Department could continue American policies (restricting immigration of refugees even beyond the restrictions imposed by the quota system) so clearly at variance with the national tradition and the object of so much criticism by numerically small but highly regarded groups of citizens representing leadership in education, religion, and the arts and sciences."

As a result of this criticism, the State Department issued new visa instructions to American consulates, which helped increase German and Austrian immigration to 17,868 in 1938. (The combined German and Austrian quotas were 27,370 per year.) Similarly, at the beginning of 1943, Britain called for an international effort in settling refugees from the Nazis. The Parliamentary Undersecretary of State for Foreign Affairs, Richard Law, remarked that "British public opinion on behalf of the Jews had risen to such a degree that the government 'could no longer remain dead to it.' " This call led to the Bermuda Conference on Refugees of April, 1943—from which no constructive proposal for aiding the refugees emerged.

It seems that while public opinion concerned with humanitarian concerns and moral considerations evoked minor, public relations changes from the government, it was never successful in effecting significant changes in policy. While the United States urged its consuls to be less stringent in granting visas, it never seriously considered raising its quota for German refugees. While England called for an international conference on behalf of the refugees, it never considered liberalizing its Palestine policy, expressed in the White Paper of 1939, which choked off immigration of Jews to that haven.

How effective can public opinion expressed through newspapers, petitions, rallies, etc. ever be in influencing the government's evaluation of our national interest? What effect did public opinion have on United States policy in Vietnam? Could American Jews and non-Jews have been more effective with more dramatic methods of protest against our State Department's callous attitude toward Jewish victims of Nazism, such as hunger strikes, civil disobedience, and other methods used in civil rights demonstrations? To what extent should the government be influenced by public opinion? To what extent should it mold it?

4. World Opinion
How much influence does world opinion have in influencing the conduct of a particular nation? Morse indicates that Germany, especially in the early years of Hitler's rule, was at times responsive to world opinion and diplomatic protests. The first weeks after Hitler came to power were characterized by brutal legislative and physcial assaults on the Jews and a general

reign of terror. This was widely publicized in American newspapers which reacted strongly.

Said the *Syracuse Post-Standard:* The whole weight of world disapproval should be summoned to stop this tragic situation, to impress upon the present rulers of Germany that the world will not permit a return to the dark ages.

The *Providence Journal* agreed: If there ever was a time in recent history for marshalling world public opinion against such brutality, such a time is now.

The *Daily Oklahoman* observed: Humanity, to say nothing of Christian duty, would call insistently for an American protest.

They were joined by a growing chorus of protest.

The American Consul General in Berlin, George Messermith, reported that the Nazis were sensitive to unfavorable publicity in other countries. The United States, however, protested only the molesting of a few American citizens who happened to be beaten up by storm troopers.

"Secretary of State Cordell Hull notified the American Embassy in Berlin that public opinion in the United States was alarmed at press reports about the mistreatment of Jews. The government was now under heavy pressure to make a formal protest to Germany. 'I am of the opinion,' wrote the secretary, 'that outside intercession has rarely produced the results desired and has frequently aggravated the situation.'

"With varying phrasing this was to be the central theme of American policy toward Nazi Germany for years to come."

When do foreign countries have the right, or the moral obligation, to protest about the internal affairs of another nation? Should the United States have protested Germany's treatment of its Jews in 1933? Should our government denounce the treatment of the natives in South Africa? Do other countries have the right to protest our own treatment of Blacks today? What is the effect of such protests? What effect did world opinion have on our policy in Vietnam? On the treatment of Jews in the Soviet Union and other Communist countries? On the Soviet Union's invasion of Afghanistan? Can large nations offend the "conscience of the world" with impunity, while small nations are punished? Is there truly a "conscience of the world"?

5. German Guilt

Morse vigorously refutes the claim that most Germans did not really know what was happening to the Jews. A *New York Times* article of March 20, 1933, described numerous instances of brutality against Jews and ended with the observation that "the feature of all this which most impresses Americans seems to be the comparative indifference displayed by the German people as a whole." Morse makes his point emphatically:

"From the advent of the Hitler onslaught, the actions taken against the Jews were carried out with the full knowledge of the German public. Communities vied with one another to proclaim restrictions against Jews; they competed for the honor of posting signs at town limits boasting that they excluded Jews, refused to sell them real estate or, most triumphant of all, were *judenfrei*. From the list of those Germans who knew nothing about such Nazi activities—a list which grows longer each year—one must therefore exclude the citizens of more than 50 cities in what Morse says is 'only a partial list.'

"For those citizens of the Third Reich who missed these public notices of hostility or failed to observe the disappearance of a Jewish neighbor, there were other opportunities to view Nazi anti-Semitism. These included numerous public humiliations. . . ."

The existence of the first concentration camp, Dachau, was public knowledge in Germany, as it was in other European countries and the United States, in 1933. Few Germans could have been ignorant of the anti-Jewish violence on November 10, 1938, the infamous Kristallnacht, when 195 synagogues were burned, 800 Jewish-owned shops destroyed and 7,500 looted, and 20,000 Jews arrested and taken to concentration camps. The report in *The New York Times* said:

"Beginning systematically in the early morning hours in almost every town and city in the country, the wrecking, looting, and burning continued all day. Huge but mostly silent crowds looked on and the police confined themselves to regulating traffic and making wholesale arrests of Jews 'for their own protection.' "

How much of the guilt is shared by the "huge but mostly silent crowds" which "looked on"? What should be our attitude toward the German people today—toward the older Germans who were part of those crowds, toward the younger Germans who were born after the war? Can a *people* be held collectively guilty? For how long? Was the acquiescence of the masses of Germans—acquiescence both active and passive—based on patriotism, an unwillingness to get involved, an acceptance of the government's arbitrary designation of a scapegoat—or was it motivated by a deep-seated hatred of the Jews as Jews? Are "huge but mostly silent crowds" in our country today looking on at actions for which we may at some future time be held accountable?

6. Implications for the Future

"The War Refugee Board, established by the United States in 1944, represented a small gesture of atonement by a nation whose apathy and inaction were exploited by Adolf Hitler. As he moved systematically toward the total destruction of the Jews, the government and the people of the United States remained bystanders. Oblivious to the evidence which poured from official and unofficial sources, Americans went about their business unmoved and unconcerned. Those who tried to awaken the nation were dismissed as alarmists, cranks, or Zionists. Many Jews were as disinterested as their Christian countrymen. The bystanders to cruelty became bystanders to genocide.

"The Holocaust has ended. The Six Million lie in nameless graves. But what of the future? Is genocide now unthinkable, or are potential victims somewhere in the world going about their business, devoted to their children, aspiring to a better life, unaware of a gathering threat?

"Who are the potential victims? Who are the bystanders?"

How can Jews best honor the memory of the Six Million? What can we learn from their experience and from the experience of Jews who lived through those times in the United States? Have our actions in behalf of the Jews in the Soviet Union shown that we have learned from the lessons of 1933–45? Or will we one day beat our breasts for not having done more and say kaddish for them, too?

Why has the United States never ratified the Genocide Convention, which would make the extermination of an ethnic group a crime by international law. Why has this genocide convention never been invoked? Would international law make any difference? Will the world ever respond to the anguished pleas of the victims and the enraged outcries of the concerned? Or does it respond only to political interests, economic power, and military force?

These are questions every civilized society must face.

7. *Sympathy vs. Action*

In early 1939, a Gallup poll revealed that 94 percent of Americans disapproved of the German treatment of Jews and 97 percent disapproved of the German treatment of Catholics. A few months later, *Fortune* published the results of a public opinion poll in which respondents had been asked, "If you were a member of Congress, would you vote 'yes' or 'no' on a bill to open the doors of the United States to a larger number of European refugees than now admitted under our immigration quotas?" The results: 83 percent said no; 8.3 percent said don't know; 8.7 percent said yes.

"*Fortune* reported that only 6.3 percent of the Protestants and 8.3 percent of the Catholics favored an increase in the quotas. In sharp contrast, 69.8 percent of the Jews called for larger quotas. 'Here is an American tradition put to the test,' concluded the editors of *Fortune,* 'and here it is repudiated by a majority of nearly ten to one. . . .' The answer is the more decisive because it was made at a time when public sympathy for victims of European events was presumably at its highest."

The gulf between sympathy and action, between words and

deeds, is one that many continue to point out today. How many northerners who expressed disapproval for the southern treatment of Blacks are opposed to open housing laws in their own states or would try to prevent Blacks from moving into their own neighborhoods? The surveys mentioned were taken against the background of the debate on the Wagner-Rogers bill, which would have permitted the United States to accept 20,000 refugee children in addition to the regular German quota. The bill was defeated. Would all the Americans who express sympathy for the starving children in Uganda be in favor of accepting 20,000 Ugandan refugee children in our country? (Sometimes the gulf between sympathy and action *can* be overcome. Reform Jewish congregations in the US have adopted and resettled more than 1,800 Indo-Chinese refugees, the boat people of our time, and we extended our hands to Cuban and Haitian refugees as well.)

WE MUST NEVER FORGET THE HOLOCAUST

As Jews we must never forget the Holocaust. To forget it, to let its memory fade, would be to give Hitler a posthumous victory. And yet we must be careful, even with the memory of the Holocaust. Just as it would be a sin to forget it, so is it wrong to let the Holocaust so overpower everything else that it becomes the end-all and the be-all of Jewish existence. Being Jewish is something more than suffering, pain, and persecution. If that were not so, why should any young Jew care to perpetuate the Jewish legacy? Let us not reduce Jewish history only to tears, torture, and torment. If that were all there is to it, how could we welcome converts into the Jewish fold? To suffer and bleed and die with us? Let us not use the Holocaust to fill the emotional vacuum of Jewish life, or to silence those who disagree with us by invoking the memory of the Six Million.

Judaism is a passionate commitment to life, to this world, to human values. Those Jewish values have never been more sorely needed to keep man human in a callous age.

Oliver Wendell Holmes once said: "A man should share the action and passion of his times at peril of being judged not to have lived." As Jews we must seize the moral challenges of our time at the peril of betraying God and our history, and abandoning that vision of one humanity under one God which has guided us through the centuries. One of our sages said no person can be fully human unless his heart has been broken. Our Jewish hearts were broken in every generation, including this, and we believe that one meaning of our suffering is this: *We will not stand idly by in any holocaust—against us or anybody else!*

For we Jews are not just another ethnic group or religious denomination. Our survival has been for a spiritual purpose, and our survival must have meaning today.

If, in order to survive, we must bid the world goodbye, separate ourselves from humankind, emulate the violence, the callousness, the bigotry, and the narrowness of our opponents . . . then survival is a dubious virtue. To be a Jew is to be a *goad* to the conscience of mankind, to have a heart of flesh and not of stone. To be a Jew is to be a part of the civilizing and humanizing force of the universe. To be a Jew is to defy despair, though the Messiah tarries. To be a Jew, as God told Abraham thousands of years ago, is to be part of a great and enduring people, but also to be a blessing unto all mankind.

13

THE ETHICAL WILL
A SOCIO-DRAMA

"The Ethical Will" is an updated version of "The Three Sons"—a technique to discuss the qualities which make a person a good Jew. The program does not require a trained discussion leader. The following instructions may be helpful:

1. Do not undertake this discussion with a group larger than 20–25 participants. In case of a large audience, each group of 20–25 conducts its own discussion and all come together again at the end to compare decisions.

2. No warm-up or prelude is necessary. The chairperson begins immediately with page 1.

3. Following the reading of The Ethical Will, two alternate procedures are available:

a. Following the selection of a chairperson, a straw vote can be taken among the audience, followed by discussion. The straw vote should be by closed ballot.

b. Following the selection of a chairperson, three members of the group speak 1–2 minutes each, justifying their claims to be worthy of the money. Then the straw vote can be taken.

4. Discussion should be limited to 40 minutes. At the close of

discussion, a final vote by secret ballot should be taken and the results announced.

THE TESTAMENT

Jacob Goodman, a prominent Jewish businessman, died last week. He left a strange will:

"Know all persons by these testaments, etc., that I leave all my inheritance to whichever one of my children shall be deemed to be the best Jew. My attorney shall select a committee of representative Jews to make this determination. If this committee decides that none of my children is worthy to be called a good Jew, or if the committee cannot agree on a selection, my estate is to be divided equally among the following philanthropies. . . ."

This much of the will is relevant. You have been selected as the committee to make the decision required. I hope you will pay close attention as I present to you the necessary information about Marshall, Donald, and Susan.

THE CHARACTERS

MARSHALL GOODMAN is the oldest and wealthiest of the Goodman children. He owns and operates several large businesses. He is married and has three grown children. Marshall is a member of the synagogue and the largest contributor to the synagogue and to the United Jewish Appeal. He does not often attend services, but he did send his three children to a religious school. He is a supporter of interfaith activities and was honored by the National Conference of Christians and Jews for his contributions to brotherhood. He was recently named in a business scandal. A nursing home for aged Jews was disclosed by the press as a "rip-off of public funds, an unsanitary and despicable dumping ground and warehouse for the aged." Marshall, the largest investor in the home, admitted that he had not paid sufficient attention to the day-to-day operations of the business and promised to rectify the conditions at the home.

DONALD GOODMAN, the second son, is an intellectual and a scholar. He teaches philosophy at the State University and grew up at a time of great social activism. He had been involved in civil rights activities, was active against the Vietnam War, works for public education, etc. Donald does not belong to a synagogue because he considers himself an atheist. When he was a boy, his best friend died and he vehemently declared that there is no God. His children do not go to religious school. However, he has always cared deeply about the Jewish people and especially Israel. Following the Yom Kippur War, he made aliyah and lived on a kibbutz in the Negev for a year. Deciding he could do more for Israel in the United States, he returned and became a leader in political and fund-raising causes for Israel and in the struggle for the rights of the Soviet Jews. Donald is married to a non-Jewish woman. When a rabbi refused to officiate at his wedding unless Gail first converted to Judaism, Donald denounced him as a "bigot" and accused him of "religious intolerance."

SUSAN GOODMAN, the youngest child, is married to a Jewish man and has one daughter. As a teenager, Susan had been a NFTY leader, serving as a regional officer, and spent one summer in a Mitzvah Corps project. When she went to college, she was far away from home for the first time and became very lonely and frightened. She became involved with a group of students who were using drugs. One day, while sitting on the mall somewhat spaced out, she was approached by a friendly and warm classmate who invited her to a retreat in the country. Within a week, she had become a member of an exotic cult, signing away her possessions and subscribing completely to the teachings of the "master." After six months, her family located her and she agreed to be "deprogrammed." Thereafter, she went to see the family rabbi and, noting her need for authority and discipline, he suggested she study at a yeshiva. She did and ultimately became a devout Orthodox Jew. Now she will not go to the homes of other members of the family because they do not keep kosher; she believes they are not "real, Torah-true, observant Jews." They regard her as one who traded one fanaticism for another. Susan met her husband at the yeshiva. They both devote themselves to a life of Jewish study and observance and hope to have six or seven children. When asked about zero population growth, Susan retorts that it cannot apply to Jews in the wake of the Holocaust and that the Torah commands us to "be fruitful and multiply."